The Ultimate
Uncheese
Cookbook

Jo Stepaniak

Book Publishing Company
Summertown, Tennessee

Cover art: Linda Paul (www.lindapaul.com)
Cover design: Warren Jefferson
Interior design: Gwynelle Dismukes
Photography: Warren Jefferson
Food stylist: Barbara Bloomfield

Published in the United States by
Book Publishing Company
P.O. Box 99
Summertown, TN 38483
1–888–260–8458 www.bookpubco.com

Printed in Canada

ISBN10 1–57067–151–6
ISBN13 978–1–57067–151–7

16 15 14 13 12   12 11 10 9 8

Stepaniak, Jo, 1954–
   The ultimate uncheese cookbook / by Jo Stepaniak.
      p. cm.
   ISBN 1–57067–151–6
  1. Milk-free diet--Recipes. 2. Cookery (Tofu) I. Title.

RM234.5.S739 2003
641.5'63--dc22   2003015951

Calculations for the nutritional analyses in this book are based on the average number of servings listed with the recipes and the average amount of an ingredient if a range is called for. Calculations are rounded up to the nearest gram. If two options for an ingredient are listed, the first one is used. Not included are fat used for frying (unless the amount is specified in the recipe), optional ingredients, or serving suggestions.

The Book Publishing Co. is committed to preserving ancient forests and natural resources. We chose to print this title on paper that is 100% postconsumer recycled and processed chlorine free. As a result of our paper choice, we saved the following natural resources:

64 trees
3,315 pounds of solid waste
25,813 gallons of water
6,219 pounds of greenhouse gases
20 million BTU of net energy

We are a member of Green Press Initiative. For more information about Green Press Initiative visit: www.greenpressinitiative.org. Paper calculations from Environmental Defense www.papercalculator.org.

Contents

UNCHEESE VERSUS CHEESE

by Vesanto Melina, MS, RD

People often say, "I could easily give up dairy products–except for cheese." It's understandable. Those unique flavors and that distinctive nip are hard to dismiss. And yet we have compelling reasons to search for alternatives. For some, these reasons involve allergy or food intolerance; others are concerned about how calves and cows are exploited in the creation of cheese. Some, aware of the damage done by the dairy industry to soil, water, and air, choose to minimize their environmental footprint. Still others are concerned about the high fat content of dairy products, such as cheese, and the effects of various components of cow's milk on their health.

One group that is worried about the effect of fatty foods such as cheese is New York City's Education Department. Acknowledging that obesity is "epidemic" among schoolchildren, the Department is reducing the fat content in the 800,000 meals it serves daily. A recent study showed that according to the Centers for Disease Control guidelines, almost 20 percent of third graders and 21 percent of sixth graders in New York City are obese. In some neighborhoods, almost 15 percent of the population has diabetes, a condition related to diet and lack of exercise.

After trying to "reformulate" macaroni and cheese with more nutritious ingredients, the Department has decided to cut back on this lunchroom staple and similar dishes. In typical "mac and cheese," about half the calories come from fat. Compare this with Cheez–A–Roni (page 90), in which just 21 percent of the calories come from fats. Not only are the healthful ingredients in Cheez–A–Roni packed with B vitamins, vitamin E, iron, and zinc, this delicious entrée is cholesterol–free!

Cow's milk has been a part of the diet for some, but not by any means all, population groups for thousands of years. How did dairy products come to be an *essential food group* for North Americans?

DAIRY AND POLITICS

The first North American food guide was published by the U.S. Department of Agriculture (USDA) in 1916. This guide contained a recommendation to include 10 percent of one's daily calories from milk, which translated to one cup of milk daily. By the 1930s, a family food-buying guide advised each American to consume two cups of milk daily. From the 1940s on, the recommendation for dairy switched to "milk and milk products." From that time forward, USDA food guides became a familiar educational and meal-planning tool in the United States. The dairy industry lobbied to ensure its strong presence on every version of the guide, with its products taking up as much as 25 percent of the area where recommended food groups were shown. Then the industry did its best to get its message to every school child and adult in America, as it continues to do today.

It has long concerned some nutritionists that the USDA has a dual role: on one hand to provide nutrition advice to the public, and on the other to ensure the success of American agriculture. There was an understandable desire for economic recovery from the depression and for agricultural prosperity after the war. This emphasis persists today amidst even more powerful lobbying from the dairy and meat industries. Accordingly, we should take this into account when evaluating health advice from the USDA.

In 1943, the National Research Council of the National Academy of Sciences released the first recommended dietary allowances (RDAs). The RDAs focused attention on recommended intakes for specific nutrients: minerals such as calcium, and vitamins such as riboflavin. These recommended intakes are "best guesses" by a group of scientific experts and include large safety margins. The RDAs have become a gold standard against which diets can be judged.

Through the first half of the twentieth century, and beyond, the science of nutrition was focused on overcoming deficiencies of various nutrients, for example on getting enough protein. Food guides reflected this concern. Yet for decades, awareness had been mounting that deficiency was not the whole story. Recognition was growing that excesses of fatty, high-protein, and salty foods could also be a problem, leading to devastating and deadly chronic diseases: coronary artery disease, various cancers, diabetes, strokes, obesity, and osteoporosis.

The 1992 pyramid was the first food guide to consider the harmful effects of over nutrition. Yet the original pyramid met such heavy pressure from food industry lobbyists, for example from The National Cattlemen's Association, that it was not released for a year, and not in its original, more health-oriented form.

Dr. Marion Nestle, the chair of New York University's Department of Nutrition and Food Studies, managed the production of the first (and only) Surgeon General's Report on Nutrition and Health in 1988. In her book *Food Politics: How the Food Industry Influences Nutrition and Health* (University of California Press, 2002) she provides examples of her experience with the food industry's influence on government dietary guidelines. "My first day on the job, I was given the rules: No matter what the research indicated, the report could not recommend 'eat less meat' as a way to reduce intake of saturated fat... The producers of food that might be affected by such advice would complain to their beneficiaries in Congress, and the report would never be published."

Not only does the U.S. Government encourage our use of dairy products through massive national nutrition education programs, it provides direct and indirect economic support to agricultural systems that produce milk, meat, and other similar commodities. One reason for the low cost of such foods is the multitude of subsidies, often in areas that escape our detection. Taxpayers support production quotas, market quotas, import restrictions, deficiency payments, lower tax rates, low-cost land leases, land management, water rights, marketing programs, and promotion programs. In a four-year period, from 1996 to 2000, agricultural subsidies took a 55 percent leap from about $18 billion to $28 billion annually.

DAIRY INDUSTRY: INFLUENCES FROM BIRTH

From the day we emerge from the womb, the dairy industry has its advertising energy enthusiastically focused on meeting our nutritional needs. It stands ready with a free diaper bag and samples of free cow's milk–based formula. It has the American Academy of Family Physicians convinced that "You shouldn't feel bad if you are unable or choose not to breast feed" and that "Your family doctor will usually recommend a formula made from cow's milk."

Can the USDA be fully trusted to release guidelines that fairly reflect the best science? For its Dietary Guidelines 2000, the Advisory Committee included such industry affiliations as:

- Dannon Company (dairy products, yogurt)
- National Dairy Council
- National Dairy Promotion and Research Board
- Mead Johnson Nutritionals (milk-based infant formulas)
- Nestlé (milk-based formulas, condensed milk, and ice cream)
- Slim-fast (milk-based diet products)

For low-income moms enrolled in the federally funded WIC program (also known as the Special Supplemental Nutrition Program for Women, Infants, and Children), the formulas provided automatically are those made from cow's milk. The WIC program serves pregnant, postpartum, and breastfeeding women; infants; and children up to five years of age who are considered to be at nutritional risk and whose family income is below state standards. It allows the purchase of dairy-based infant formula, cow's milk, and cheese. Soy-based alternatives are not so easy to obtain through the program. The dairy industry, which helped create this program, is fighting hard against proposed changes that will introduce a wider range of fruits, vegetables, legumes, and alternatives to dairy products. Yet the changes are reasonable and long overdue as the population served by WIC programs is weighted towards African American and Hispanic people with high rates of lactose intolerance and difficulty in digesting dairy products.

> Lactose intolerance, sometimes referred to as lactase nonpersistence, is the inability to digest the sugar present in milk and dairy products. Lactose is found only in the milk of mammals, not in plant foods.

By the time children reach school age, they encounter cow's milk and cheese as cornerstones of the National School Lunch Program, including about five billion half-pints of milk that are annually served in school nutrition programs. This emphasis in the menu is not surprising. It fits right in with what they'll learn in class: that cow's milk and its products are essential to the human diet.

In the 1940s and '50s, the *Guide to Good Eating*, produced by the National Dairy Council, was used to teach the fundamentals of nutrition in elementary schools across the continent. The dairy industry has maintained a foothold in educational programs ever since. This guide and its successors presented dairy products as one of four, and later five, food groups that we require each day.

Today the USDA's "Food Guide Pyramid" recommends two to three servings per day from the Milk, Yogurt, and Cheese Group. The current *Guide to Good Eating*, distributed to schools, increases the number of servings from the Milk Group to two to four daily. The dairy industry provides schools with nutrient comparison cards, guides for athletic coaches, materials on sports nutrition and weight management, guides to restaurant eating, daily food and activity journals, and posters for classroom walls or to take home and put on the refrigerator. The industry's 2003 Unified Marketing Plan specifically targets children ages six to twelve and their mothers.

For all ages, the dairy industry hammers out the message that we require cow's milk in one form or another. Billboards and magazine advertisements ask: "Got Milk?" Dozens of celebrities have been inducted into the Milk Mustache campaign. One focus of this campaign is members of ethnic groups who are known to have high levels of lactose intolerance. Mustache wearers include Hispanics, such as Freddie Prinze, Jr. and Latin heartthrob Marc Anthony; African Americans, such as Whoopi Goldberg, Spike Lee, Tyra Banks, Terrell Davis, Marion Jones, Nelly, and Venus and Serena Williams; and Asians, such as Jackie Chan, Zhang Ziyi, and Kristi Yamaguchi.

John Robbins, author of *Diet for a New America* (H. J. Kramer, 1987, 1998) and *The Food Revolution* (Conari Press, 2001), accuses the USDA of nutritional racism. "The federal government currently recommends that all U.S. children drink milk every day—including the 70 percent of African Americans, 95 percent of Native Americans, 60 percent of Hispanic Americans, and 90 percent of Asian Americans who are lactose intolerant. Federal guidelines continue to advocate dairy products as the primary source of calcium, ignoring the fact that most people of color experience nausea, intestinal gas, bloating, abdominal cramps and diarrhea when they eat milk, cheese, or other dairy products. Current USDA dietary guidelines tell all Americans they should eat two to three servings of milk products every day. This benefits the dairy industry, but it is an injustice to people of color, who are not told that there are many other foods (including green leafy vegetables, soymilk, and tofu) that are excellent sources of calcium."

The dairy industry makes its presence known at conventions of dietitians, physicians, and other health professionals, and has done an effective job of convincing many of these opinion leaders that cow's milk is essential to human health.

CALCIUM, BONES, AND LIFESTYLE

Milk is touted (by the dairy industry) for preventing osteoporosis, yet does it? The Harvard Nurses' Health Study, which followed more than 75,000 women for twelve years, showed no protective effect of increased milk consumption on fracture risk. In fact, increased intake of calcium from dairy products was associated with a higher fracture risk. An Australian study showed the same results. Many studies, such as those by Cumming and Huang, also found no protective effect of dairy calcium on bone.

A review in the *American Journal of Clinical Nutrition* by Weinsier states that over-all the research fails to support a conclusion that daily consumption of dairy products improves bone health. Many studies have been poorly designed and ethnic groups, men, and several age groups of women are poorly represented in the study populations. Despite the fact that most were financed by the dairy industry, more than half of the studies showed no benefit to bone health from milk products. In those that showed benefits, the effects were miniscule. Some studies showed adverse effects. In other words, these foods may add some calcium to our diets, but this benefit is undermined by factors that increase our calcium losses.

There are many flaws in relying on dairy products to keep our bones strong. Dairy products are not essential, are not our only sources of dietary calcium, and are not ideal calcium sources for numerous reasons. Furthermore, many lifestyle factors beyond calcium intake are responsible for lifelong bone health.

Relying on this single mineral, calcium, to build bones and prevent osteoporosis is like trying to play baseball with only a pitcher on your team. We need other members of the bone health team, on bases, behind the plate, and in key spots out in the field. The team includes calcium, vitamin D, protein, boron, copper, fluoride, magnesium, manganese, potassium, zinc, and vitamins B_6, B_{12}, C, K, and folic acid. Physical activity, could take the powerful position of "team coach," as it supports bone strength and helps us hold on to the minerals we have in our skeleton.

> **W**hat is our best course of action? We decrease our risk of osteoporosis by:
>
> • reducing dietary factors that leach calcium from the bones, primarily sodium and animal protein,
> • consuming an overall balanced diet of bone building nutrients, and
> • taking part in regular exercise, especially weight-bearing exercise.

MILK: DOES IT DO A BODY GOOD?

There are many reasons why cow's milk is not "nature's perfect food"–except for baby calves. For a great many humans, dairy products are far from ideal.

Cheese, ice cream, milk, butter, and yogurt contribute significant amounts of cholesterol, fat, and saturated fat to the diet. Diets high in fat and saturated fat can increase the risk of several chronic diseases, including cardiovascular disease. American milk consumption dropped from an average of 25.5 gallons of whole milk per person per year (which works out to 1⅛ cups per day) in 1970 to about one-third that amount by 1997 (8.5 gallons per person). But all the original dairy fat and more were introduced back via the immense American appetite for cheese, in fat-laden foods such as pizza. Whereas annual U.S. sales for milk now total about $11 billion, cheese sales bring the dairy industry over $16 billion each year.

There are a number of links between milk products and cancer. The hormone in dairy products known as IGF-1, or insulin-like growth factor, helps promote cell division and rapid weight gain in calves (from 60 to 600 pounds). IGF-1 also has been shown to accelerate the growth of cancer tumors. This hormone is particularly high in cows injected with recombinant bovine growth hormone (rBGH), a genetically engineered hormone that increases milk production and has been permitted in U.S. dairy herds since 1985. When we consume dairy products from cows whose fodder was grown with pesticides and herbicides, which is the case unless one chooses organic products, these contaminants accumulate in our fatty tissues. Research has shown links between higher levels of these contaminants and increased incidence of cancer. Saturated animal fat itself may be associated with cancers of the breast, endometrium, prostate, lung, colon, and rectum.

Links have also been found between childhood-onset (Type I) diabetes and early consumption of dairy products. Karjalainen, reporting in the *New England Journal of Medicine*, and other researchers, found that a specific dairy protein sparks an auto-immune reaction that is believed to destroy the insulin-producing cells of the pancreas in some children. The evidence incriminating cow's milk consumption in the cause of Type-1 diabetes is sufficient to cause the American Academy of Pediatrics to issue warnings (see box, right).

> • Early exposure of infants to cow's milk protein may be an important factor in the initiation of the beta cell (insulin-producing cells of the pancreas) destructive process in some individuals.
>
> • The avoidance of cow's milk protein for the first several months of life may reduce the later development of IDDM or delay its onset in susceptible people.

Dairy protein stimulates widespread allergies and intolerances, particularly in children. Milk contains twenty-five different proteins. Reactions to protein can affect the intestinal tract from one end to the other, as well as the nose, sinuses, inner ear, bones, joints, skin, nervous system (and therefore moods), and kidneys. One of the proteins that can trigger allergic reactions is *casein*, the protein responsible for allowing cheeses to melt and spread on pizza and in lasagne and grilled cheese sandwiches. Note that casein is present in many commercial cheese substitutes that are labeled lactose-free.

Another reason to limit dairy products is that cow's milk is very low in iron and can inhibit the absorption of iron from other foods by 50 percent or more. In young infants, cow's milk is the leading cause of iron deficiency anemia, as specific proteins can irritate the lining of the gastrointestinal tract, causing blood loss in the stools. The American Academy of Pediatrics recommends that infants below one year of age not be given cow's milk. It stands to reason that others, such as women and children, who are susceptible to iron deficiency anemia, avoid making dairy products a major part of their diet.

Further concerns that arise are:

- Links between use of cows' milk by some breastfeeding mothers and the possibility of colic in their infants. It seems that antibodies from the cow can pass through the mother's bloodstream into her breast milk and to the baby.

- Possible connection between Crohn's disease and milk consumption. The cause may be insufficient pasteurization to destroy a microorganism called MAP (Mycobacterium avium subspecies paratuberculosis).

- Constipation. In a study of 65 severely constipated children, published in the *New England Journal of Medicine*, 68 percent of the children found relief of their constipation when cow's milk was removed from their diets. When cow's milk was reintroduced into their diets eight to twelve months later, all developed constipation within five to ten days.

DO WE NEED DAIRY PRODUCTS?

Are dairy products really an essential food group for humans? What we truly require for good health is an assortment of nutrients, such as protein, calcium, and riboflavin. All of these, and other important nutrients in milk, can be obtained from an immense variety of foods, without the associated saturated fat, cholesterol, and various contaminants that are found in dairy products.

PROTEIN

Though animal products are sometimes considered to be synonymous with protein foods, protein is widely distributed in plant foods, with the exceptions of highly refined items such as sugar, fats, and oils. Let's compare the percentage of calories from protein, fat and carbohydrate in various foods in table 1 (page 16) with the ranges that are recommended for our overall diet, shown on the bottom line of the table. Some grains, alone, fit the recommended range very closely. We can see that an assortment of plant foods will easily give us a balance of protein, fat, and carbohydrate that is within the recommended range. (For more on protein, see *Becoming Vegetarian*, V. Melina and B. Davis, Book Publishing Co., Summertown, TN).

From plants foods we can get optimal amounts of protein, including every one of the essential amino acids that are the building blocks of our body proteins.

CALCIUM

Though advertising from the dairy industry tries to convince us that it is virtually impossible to get enough calcium in our diets without dairy products, in truth this mineral is present in a great many plant foods (see table 1, page 16).

It's not just the amount of calcium in foods that matters; the ease with which we can absorb this mineral is also an important factor. Research by Dr. Connie Weaver of Purdue University and others gives us an idea how much calcium we can expect to absorb from an assortment of plant foods (table 3, page 18). Research of this type has not been done on all the plant sources of calcium available to us. However, it is clear that we can readily absorb calcium from many foods, not just from dairy products.

Here are a few examples of the roles and our dietary sources of bone team members. **Vitamin C**, found in fruits and vegetables, helps build strengthening cross-links between molecules of the bone protein known as collagen. **Vitamin K**, from leafy greens, binds calcium to three types of protein that make up bone structure. **Boron**, a mineral in apples and other fruits, flaxseeds, nuts, vegetables, and legumes, plays a role in preventing calcium loss and may support the action of vitamin D. **Vitamin D** is essential for absorbing calcium in the intestine, reducing losses of this mineral through the urine, and storing it in bones. Note that vitamin D is added not just to cow's milk but also to fortified soymilk and rice milk. **Magnesium** is another mineral present in our bones; it comes to us from leafy greens and other vegetables, whole grains, nuts, seeds, legumes, and fruits. Diets high in fruit are associated with greater bone density. This is believed to be related to the high potassium content of fruits, as well as their contribution of other vitamins and minerals.

BENEFITS OF UNCHEESES

The uncheeses you'll find in this book can make a tremendous contribution to your well-being. Look at the nutritional analyses that accompany each recipe and you'll see the nutrients provided by each: vitamins, minerals, fiber, and plant protein.

Those made with Red Star Vegetarian Support Formula nutritional yeast provide vitamin B_{12}. Riboflavin comes from nutritional yeast, fortified soymilk, leafy green vegetables, sea vegetables, green vegetables such as asparagus, mushrooms , sweet potatoes, beans, peas, and lentils, almonds, peanuts, whole grains, and whole and enriched grain products. Instead of decreasing iron absorption, uncheeses made with beans, soy products, nuts, and seeds contribute iron to our diets. The nuts, seeds, beans, and vegetables in uncheeses are rich in fiber, whereas cheeses made from cow's milk contain no fiber at all. Recipes with walnuts, such as Besto Pesto (page 44) and the Raw Nut Crust (page 180), provide essential omega–3 fatty acids.

In addition, because the ingredients are plant foods, these uncheese recipes are rich in naturally occurring plant chemicals known as *phytochemicals* (phyto means "plant"). The beneficial effects of these substances are remarkable. There are thousands of phytochemicals. They are abundant in garlic, tomatoes, broccoli, and a host of other white, red, green, yellow, and orange vegetables; seasonings such as turmeric, cumin, dill, and cilantro; whole grains; and nuts, seeds, and soyfoods. Many phytochemicals are powerful antioxidants, helping to quench destructive free radicals. Others have potent anti–cancer activity, blocking cell division and ridding our bodies of carcinogens. Phytochemicals work to protect us against heart disease and reduce cholesterol production, blood pressure, blood clot formation, and damage to blood vessel walls. Phytoestrogens (plant estrogens) can block the destructive action of the potent form of estrogen and may reduce our risk of osteoporosis and certain types of hormone dependent cancers. Some phytochemicals have powerful anti–inflammatory activity; others support our immune systems or protect against viral, bacterial, fungal, or yeast infections.

Not only do the uncheeses in this book have superior flavor compared to commercial cheese substitutes, they are free of the milk proteins and lactose that cause an assortment of uncomfortable and unpleasant reactions in so many people. Contrasted with artery clogging cheeses made from cow's milk, you'll find most uncheeses are low in fat and saturated fat, and all are cholesterol–free. They're lower in sodium too. Just take a look at the comparison chart on page 19.

So try out Cheez–a–Roni, Gooda Cheez, Crock Cheez, and Gee Whiz Spread (four of my favorites) and get ready for true taste treats!

(See page 183 for Web sites and other references for this section.)

GETTING CALCIUM FROM PLANT FOODS

Greens. Greens are among our best bone-builders, for reasons that extend beyond their calcium content and excellent calcium absorption (see table 3). Dark leafy greens are high in vitamin K and potassium, two nutrients that play essential roles in helping our bone-building cells perform their tasks. Some that are good sources of easily absorbed calcium are bok choy, broccoli, collards, kale, many Chinese greens (apart from Chinese spinach), okra, mustard greens, and turnip greens. The proportion of calcium we absorb from these is somewhat higher than that from cow's milk. Certain sea vegetables (commonly known as "seaweeds"), specifically hijiki (hiziki), arame, and wakame, also provide calcium. (Note that spinach, Swiss chard, beet greens, and rhubarb are not included with the high calcium foods because the calcium present is tightly bound by plant acids called *oxalates*, which inhibit calcium absorption. Thus we can absorb only about 5 to 8 percent of the calcium present.

Legumes and Soyfoods. Although all beans contain calcium, some have more than others. Good choices are white beans, black turtle beans, and soybeans. Soybeans often are eaten as cooked, dried soynuts or as the mineral-packed green soybeans known by the Japanese name *edamame*, which can be found in frozen food sections of natural food stores. Soyfoods can be very important calcium sources. Tofu is made from soymilk that is allowed to set by adding a coagulant, which in many cases is a calcium salt. Amounts of calcium vary considerably from one brand or variety to another, so check the nutrition panel on the label. Tempeh, a fermented, highly digestible soyfood originating from Indonesia, also contains calcium, though less than calcium-set tofu.

Fortified Soymilk and Rice Milk. Soymilk and rice milk are available in calcium-fortified versions, generally containing the same amount of calcium per cup as cow's milk. Like cow's milk, these fortified milks have added vitamin D, which helps us absorb the calcium. Check labels for the words "fortified" or "enriched" and read the ingredient list for a calcium salt such as tricalcium phosphate. The calcium tends to settle to the bottom of the container rather than staying in suspension, so be sure to shake the closed container well before pouring.

Almonds, Sesame Seeds, and Butters. Nuts and seeds have different nutritional features; almonds are particularly rich in calcium. Sesame seeds make a lesser contribution. Almond butter and the sesame seed butter known as *tahini* make delicious spreads for toast and sandwiches. Tahini contributes calcium to a large number of the uncheese recipes in this book.

Fruits and Calcium-fortified Juices. Dried figs make an excellent sweet treat to carry in a backpack, glove compartment, or purse. They give us an energy boost, complete with plenty of calcium, iron, potassium, and fiber. Five figs (two-thirds cup) contain about as much calcium as two-thirds cup of milk. Several types of juices—orange, grapefruit, juice blends, and fruit punch—are available in calcium-fortified versions, generally containing the same amount of calcium per cup as cow's milk.

Blackstrap Molasses. When sugar cane is stripped of all its nutrients to become white sugar, a by-product of the sugar refining industry is molasses, a rich concentrate of the minerals that were in the original plants. Molasses can be concentrated in pesticides that were sprayed on the cane fields, so choose organic brands. Barbados molasses and sorghum molasses have less than one-third the mineral content of blackstrap molasses.

Table 1: Percentage of Calories from Protein, Fat, and Carbohydrate in Plant Foods and Dairy Products			
	PROTEIN	**FAT**	**CARB**
LEGUMES: BEANS, PEAS, LENTILS, AND SOYFOODS			
Beans (anasazi, black, kidney, lima, mung, pinto, red, or white; lentils, peas (black-eyed or split)	23-30%	1-4%	67-73%
Chickpeas (garbanzo beans)	21%	14%	65%
Peanuts	15%	71%	14%
Soybeans	33%	39%	28%
Tofu, firm	40%	49%	11%
NUTS, SEEDS, AND THEIR BUTTERS			
Nuts (almonds, cashews, hazelnuts, filberts)	9-14%	68-81%	13-21%
Seeds (pumpkin, sesame, sunflower)	11-17%	71-75%	12-14%
GRAINS			
Amaranth, oats, quinoa, rye, wheat	13-18%	5-16%	67-80%
Barley, corn, millet, rice	9-11%	4-7%	82-87%
VEGETABLES			
Broccoli, salad greens, spinach	31-40%	9-11%	38-57%
Carrots, yams, baked potatoes	8%	1-3%	89-91%
Kale	22%	11%	67%
Mushrooms	32-50%	0-6%	50-62%
FRUITS			
Dates, figs, raisins	3-4%	1-2%	94-96%
Melons	5-9%	2-11%	82-93%
Oranges, raspberries, strawberries	7%	2-10%	83-91%
DAIRY PRODUCTS			
Cheddar cheese, medium	25%	74%	1%
Cow's milk, 2%	27%	35%	38%
Cow's milk, whole	21%	49%	30%
Feta cheese	21%	73%	6%
Gouda cheese	25-28%	69-73%	2%
Mozzarella cheese	26%	71%	3%
Mozzarella cheese, reduced fat	42%	53%	5%
RECOMMENDED RANGE	**10-20%**	**15-35%**	**50-70%**

Table 2: Calcium in Plant Foods and Dairy Products

FOOD AND AMOUNT	CALCIUM, MG
GREEN VEGETABLES	
Bok choy, raw, 2 cups	147
Bok choy, cooked, 1 cup	178
Broccoli, raw, 2 cups	84
Broccoli, cooked 1 cup	70-94
Chinese broccoli, cooked (88 g)	88
Chinese (Nappa) cabbage, raw, 2 cups	117
Chinese (Nappa) cabbage, cooked, 1 cup	158
Chinese cabbage flower leaves, cooked, 1 cup	478
Chinese mustard greens, cooked, 1 cup	424
Chinese okra, 1 cup	112
Collard greens, cooked, 1 cup	226
Kale, raw, 2 cups	181
Kale, cooked, 1 cup	94-179
Mustard greens, 1 cup	128
Okra, 1 cup	101
Romaine lettuce, raw, 2 cups	40
Seaweed, hijiki or arame, dry, ½ cup	100-140
Turnip greens, 2 cups	209
LEGUMES AND SOYFOODS	
Black turtle beans, cooked, 1 cup	46-120
Cranberry beans, cooked, 1 cup	94
Chick-peas (garbanzo beans), cooked, 1 cup	80
Kidney beans, cooked, 1 cup	50
Lentils, cooked, 1 cup	38
Navy beans, cooked, 1 cup	127
Pinto Beans, cooked, 1 cup	82
Red beans, cooked, 1 cup	81-85
White beans, cooked, 1 cup	226
Green soybeans, 1 cup	185
Soybeans, cooked, 1 cup	175

FOOD AND AMOUNT	CALCIUM, MG
LEGUMES AND SOYFOODS	
Soynuts, 2 ounces	113
Tofu, firm (made with calcium), ½ cup	152-336
Tofu, silken firm, ½ cup	40
Tempeh, ½ cup	92
Veggie ground round, Yves, 3 ounces	62
NONDAIRY MILKS	
Fortified soy and grain milks, ½ cup	100-250
Unfortified soy and grain milks, 1½ cup	5-10
NUTS, SEEDS, AND BUTTERS	
Almonds, ¼ cup	115
Almond butter, 3 tablespoons	130
Flaxseed, 2 tablespoons	47
Hazelnuts, ¼ cup	38
Sesame tahini, 3 tablespoons	50-63
FRUITS AND JUICES	
Figs, 5	137-197
Orange, 1 medium	52
Fortified orange juice, ½ cup	150-154
SWEETENER	
Blackstrap molasses, 1 tablespoon	176
DAIRY PRODUCTS	
Cow's milk, nonfat, 2% or whole, ½ cup	143-153
Cheese, cheddar, ¾ ounces	151
Cheese, cottage, nonfat, 2% or whole, ½ cup	67-82
Cheese, feta, ¾ ounces	104
Cheese, gouda, ¾ ounces	147
Cheese, mozzarella, ¾ ounces	75-169
Yogurt, ½ cup	156-200

Table 3: Calcium from Foods, Estimated Absorption			
Food	Calcium mg*	Percentage absorption*	Estimated Absorbable Calcium, mg
BEANS AND PRODUCTS			
Tofu with calcium, ½ cup	258	31%	80
White beans, cooked, ½ cup	113	22%	25
Pinto beans, ½ cup	45	27%	12
Red beans, ½ cup	41	24%	10
FORTIFIED BEVERAGE			
Fruit punch with calcium citrate malate, 1 cup	300	52%	156
LOW-OXALATE GREENS			
Bok choy, cooked, ½ cup	79	53%	42
Broccoli, cooked, ½ cup	35	61%	21
Chinese cabbage flower leaves, cooked, ½ cup	239	40%	95
Chinese mustard greens, cooked, ½ cup	212	40%	85
Kale, cooked, ½ cup	61	49%	30
Mustard greens, cooked, ½ cup	64	58%	37
Turnip greens, cooked, ½ cup	99	52%	51
HIGH OXALATE FOODS			
Chinese spinach, cooked, ½ cup	347	8%	29
Spinach, cooked, ½ cup	115	5%	6
Rhubarb, cooked, ½ cup	174	5%	15
NUTS AND SEEDS			
Almonds, dry roasted, 1 ounce	80	21%	18
Sesame seeds, without hulls, 1 ounce	37	21%	8
DAIRY PRODUCTS			
Cow's milk, 1 cup	300	32%	96
Cheddar cheese, 1.5 ounces	303	32%	97
Dairy yogurt, 1 cup	300	32%	96

A COMPARISON OF DAIRY CHEESES VS. UNCHEESES

Cheese	Amount	Calories	Fat (g)	Sodium (mg)	Cholesterol (mg)	Protein (g)
American cheese	1 tbsp.	35	3.0	135	9	2.1
Process cheese spread	1 tbsp.	47	3.4	218	9	2.7
Gee Whiz Spread	**1 tbsp.**	**29**	**0.8**	**36**	**0**	**2.0**
Swiss cheese	1 oz.	107	7.8	74	26	8.1
Swizz Cheez	**1 oz.**	**40**	**0.3**	**28**	**0**	**2.0**
Muenster cheese	1 oz.	104	8.5	178	27	6.6
Muenster Cheez	**1 oz.**	**40**	**2.5**	**116**	**0**	**1.0**
Colby cheese	1 oz.	112	9.1	171	27	6.7
Colby Cheez	**1 oz.**	**17**	**2.0**	**101**	**0**	**1.0**
Cream cheese	1 oz.	99	9.9	84	31	2.1
Rich Tofu Creme Cheez	**1 oz.**	**44**	**3.0**	**127**	**0**	**2.0**
Feta cheese	1 oz.	75	6.0	316	24	4
Betta Feta	**1 oz.**	**31**	**1.5**	**237**	**0**	**3.0**
Gouda cheese	1 oz.	101	7.8	232	32	7.1
Gooda Cheez	**1 oz.**	**36**	**2.0**	**96**	**0**	**2.0**
Mozzarella (whole)	1 oz.	80	6.1	106	22	5.5
Buffalo Mostarella	**1 oz.**	**30**	**1.0**	**87**	**0**	**2.0**
Parmesan (grated)	1 tbsp.	33	1.5	93	4	2.1
Parmezano Sprinkles	**1 tbsp.**	**32**	**3.0**	**47**	**0**	**2.0**
Ricotta (skim)	½ cup	171	9.8	155	38	14.0
Tofu Ricotta	**½ cup**	**156**	**8.0**	**252**	**0**	**16.0**
Brie	1 oz.	95	7.9	178	28	5.9
Brie Cheez	**1 oz.**	**37**	**2.5**	**95**	**0**	**2.0**

WHAT ARE UNCHEESES?

by Jo Stepaniak

Uncheeses are various rich-tasting mixtures of dairy-free whole foods that are made into spreads, dips, sauces, and blocks. I began creating uncheeses in the late eighties in response to the countless people who told me they could never give up dairy products because they "just couldn't live without cheese." I wanted to demonstrate that not only is it possible to live cheese-free, it can be done deliciously.

Not long after *The Uncheese Cookbook* was first released, a number of commercial manufacturers and recipe developers attempted to make similar creations and knockoffs. Nevertheless, there is nothing like the original. Most commercial cheese alternatives cannot duplicate the flavors, textures, adaptability, and control of ingredients obtainable with homemade uncheeses. This is because the recipes call for fresh, whole ingredients with flavors that are derived from real foods rather than refined starches and chemicals. These uncheeses also have withstood the test of time and the taste buds of countless eager volunteers. During the recipe development stage and throughout numerous trials, taste-testers who still ate dairy products were invited to sample the uncheeses and provide feedback. Only those recipes that received their stamp of approval are included in this book.

Before diving into the recipes, know that uncheeses are not going to be exactly like dairy cheeses, so please adjust your expectations accordingly. No animal-free substitutes can mimic dairy cheese precisely. This is because the primary protein in dairy cheese–specifically *casein* (which also may be listed as *caseinate* on product labels)–imparts the unique characteristics of meltability and stretch. Without casein, these qualities are somewhat lacking. This is why many manufacturers of soy cheeses include casein among their ingredients. These products are aimed for the lactose-intolerant market and were not specifically designed for vegans or people who are dairy allergic. This underscores the value of making your own homemade uncheeses: you control the ingredients–all of them!–and you decide exactly what goes into each recipe you prepare. If you want more or less salt, simply make the alteration. If you need to substitute a different bean or nut, go right ahead and do it. Do you have a love affair with garlic? By all means add more!

Dairy-based cheeses are "dead" foods. That is, most are cured or aged for long periods, so unlike fruits and vegetables, there is no vibrancy or "life force" remaining in them. Consequently, these types of cheeses rarely spoil, except for the occasional mold that is intentional or can be scraped away. Uncheeses, on the other hand, are made with fresh, wholesome ingredients that are brimming with vitality and nutrition. As with all fresh foods, however, they will spoil. So consume your uncheeses within seven to ten days after making them, and always store them in the refrigerator. Freezing uncheeses is not recommended, as this may alter their color, texture, and moisture content. Because uncheeses are so quick, effortless, and fun to make, you'll get the most flavor and quality if they are prepared fresh.

For this tenth anniversary edition of *The Uncheese Cookbook*, I have completely revised the recipes and added many new ones. I also have included a concise guide with each recipe for those who have food sensitivities or allergies. Now you can see at a glance if a recipe is free of gluten, soy, nuts, yeast, or corn. Throughout the book you'll also find a number of recipe variations and tips to help you meet any special dietary requirements you, your family, or your guests may have.

Rather than lackluster imitations of their dairy-based cousins, uncheeses were designed to launch our taste buds on exciting new adventures while providing the comfort of familiarity. Enjoy preparing these wholesome, natural foods. They are easy to make, health-supporting, delicious, and cruelty-free. May they bring you abundant joy, well-being, and peace of mind.

AN IMPORTANT NOTE ABOUT THE RECIPE INGREDIENTS AND EQUIPMENT

Cheese and the items made from it generally are considered to be "fast foods," and this book was conceived with that notion in mind. Simplicity, speed, and ease of preparation are the watchwords of every recipe.

Wherever possible, I have tried to use ingredients that are common and readily available. However, in order to achieve the highest nutritional value, taste, and cheese-like consistency, it was necessary to incorporate some ingredients that may not be familiar to you. The section "Ingredients That May Be New to You," starting on page 25, will introduce you to these ingredients and briefly explain their uses. Those items that are not available in your local supermarket can be found in most natural food stores or from the mail order vendors listed on page 182. Although some ingredients may seem strange at first, know that they are healthful, natural, and derived only from pure plant sources. I hope you will enjoy exploring these new foods and take advantage of the exciting opportunities they hold in store.

USING THE PROPER INGREDIENTS

In a number of recipes you'll find there is some flexibility with the ingredients. For instance, when feasible you will be given the option to use whatever flour you prefer, or with certain recipes you can choose between beans or tofu. However, if a particular ingredient is specified, it is important to use that exact ingredient. *For example, whenever fresh lemon juice is indicated, it is crucial to use only the fresh juice, as it is essential to the outcome of the recipe.* This is because fresh lemon juice has a bright, tart, tangy flavor, while bottled lemon juice is stale and bitter tasting. The musty, off-flavor of the bottled product will pervade whatever you prepare, turning what ought to be a perfectly delicious uncheese into an unsavory disaster. The same is true of the dried herbs and spices you use. The fresher your ingredients, the better your uncheese.

Dairy cheeses have one primary ingredient—whole animals' milk. The flavors vary based on the type of milk used, the enzymes that are added, and the aging and handling processes. Similarly, the key ingredients in uncheeses are minimal, straightforward, and uncomplicated. Consequently, only small variations in seasonings can have a huge impact on the final flavors. Although these uncheese recipes have been tested many times (and, yes, we even tested them on folks who eat dairy!), there's no way to account for the wide variations in what appeals to people. If you find some of the herbs or spices in certain recipes unpalatable, feel free to adjust, substitute, or omit them.

WHAT IF I DON'T LIKE NUTRITIONAL YEAST?

Although most people find nutritional yeast delicious at first bite, there are some on whom the flavor has to grow. Depending on your palate, nutritional yeast could taste somewhat sharp or bitter. These sensations also are associated with dairy cheese, so it is fitting that they are linked with uncheeses too. If you were never fond of the pungent aroma and assertive taste of many dairy cheeses, you may need a little time to get used to the flavor of nutritional yeast in uncheeses.

Of course, there are some folks who simply do not like nutritional yeast. Although nutritional yeast is integral to most uncheese recipes, one way to curb the taste of it is to replace the water called for in a recipe with plain, unsweetened soymilk. The rich, gentle flavor of soymilk can help "soften" the sharp taste of nutritional yeast and make it more appetizing. Another option is to add a tablespoon or two of olive oil (or organic canola or safflower oil) to a recipe instead of or in addition to the soymilk. A little added fat (in the form of soymilk, vegetable oil, or nut or seed butter) helps mellow bitter flavors and will impart an even richer, creamier taste. (To learn more about nutritional yeast, please see page 32.)

Keep in mind that strong, pungent tastes and aromas are characteristic of naturally aged cheeses. This is true of uncheeses as well, but when you make your own plant-based "cheez," you control what goes into it every time. You can tweak the recipes to suit your individual taste. That is the beauty of making uncheeses at home.

WHAT ABOUT GLUTEN-INTOLERANCE OR OTHER FOOD SENSITIVITIES?

I have endeavored to make my uncheese recipes suitable for almost everyone, regardless of dietary restrictions. In many recipes, one or two options will be listed for ingredients that are common food allergens or sensitivity triggers. This way you can customize the recipes to your specific requirements and see at a glance if a recipe will be appropriate for you.

The allergy triggers that are not contained in particular recipes will be listed in a box like the one at right. Recipes that do not contain gluten or include gluten-free options will be designated gluten free in the box. Ingredients that commonly contain gluten (such as vanilla extract) will not be marked as such. You will need to use an appropriate gluten-free brand for these types of ingredients.

FREE
OF:
GLUTEN
SOY
NUTS
YEAST
CORN

Recipes will be marked free of soy if they contain no soy products or if soy-free alternatives are specified in the ingredient list.

Those recipes that do not contain tree nuts will be marked nut free. Some of these recipes might contain sesame tahini, however. If this is the case, there will be a note beneath the allergen-free designations alerting you to this fact. Most tahini is processed in manufacturing plants that also process other nut and seed butters. It is possible that traces of these nuts may be in your tahini, depending on the brand you purchase. Please contact the manufacturer directly if you have any concern about whether or not a product is suitable for you.

Because a large number uncheeses derive their cheesy taste from nutritional yeast, many of the recipes do contain yeast. Those that are yeast free will be indicated. Some recipes that are otherwise yeast free might contain vinegar, miso, or another fermented food. These will be specified in a note beneath the allergen-free box. If you cannot have fermented foods, please carefully review the ingredient list for each recipe before proceeding.

The recipes that are free of corn will be marked as such. If you are sensitive to corn and wish to prepare a recipe calling for packaged ingredients that might contain corn derivatives, be sure to select a suitable corn-free brand.

ABOUT BLENDING AND PROCESSING

Whenever an uncheese recipe specifies using a food processor, be sure to use one that is fitted with a metal blade to achieve the best results. A significant number of the recipes call for processing different food combinations in a blender. This is necessary to effectively replicate the creamy taste and velvety texture of many familiar dairy products. With blended recipes, it is essential to process the mixtures long enough so they form a completely smooth sauce or purée. This may require several minutes of high speed blending and usually will necessitate stopping the blender occasionally to scrape down the sides of the container and stir the contents. It is well worth investing in a sturdy and powerful blender, as it will speed up your preparation time and provide smoother, more consistent results.

A number of uncheese recipes may need to be processed in batches, depending on the capacity of your blender jar. This is because the size of blender containers vary among manufacturers. Take this into consideration when processing large quantities of food. Don't overfill your blender jar; always provide a bit of "breathing room" in the top. Blended mixtures temporarily expand with air during processing. With some extra space in the jar, food can move freely and won't be pushed out under the lid. It is a wise practice to start with a smaller quantity of food in your blender and then add more if there is sufficient room.

Hot liquids release a surprising amount of steam when they are blended, and this can force the lid to pop off. The heat could even crack the blender jar if it is not heat resistant or thick enough. As a precautionary measure, fill the blender only halfway when processing hot liquids and foods, and use a kitchen towel to hold the lid slightly ajar to allow a little steam to escape.

For the best outcome, always use the type of equipment specified in each recipe. Having both a food processor and blender on hand will ensure optimum results and make preparation of your uncheeses a breeze.

INGREDIENTS THAT MAY BE NEW TO YOU

Several indispensable ingredients are regularly used in the wide assortment of uncheeses included in this book. This makes it simple to stock the pantry with all the uncheese staples you'll need and allows you to prepare uncheeses on very short notice.

Why are similar ingredients used in many of the recipes? If we consider the primary component of dairy cheese–animal milk–we notice that this single ingredient takes on a multitude of gradations of flavors and textures depending on the treatment it receives, such as the temperature at which it is cured, how long it is aged, or what type of animal milk is used. Although there are scores of dairy cheeses, we distinguish the differences among them due to the nuances that make each one distinctive.

The same is true of uncheeses: primary ingredients are given slightly different treatments to produce subtle but unique properties and flavors. The judicious application of herbs, spices, and other seasonings, as well as modifications to the type and quantity of particular foundation ingredients used, will result in a wide variety of delicious possibilities.

Here is a list of important ingredients to have on hand so you can make any uncheese in a snap.

• **Agar flakes:** Also known as *agar-agar* and *kanten*, this bland, odorless sea vegetable is a natural thickener and an excellent substitute for gelatin, which is made from animal products. Agar is available in three forms: sticks, flakes, and powder. It can be found in natural food stores in the macrobiotic section or along-side other sea vegetables. Asian markets frequently carry agar sticks and powder, often at a reasonable price. To make flakes from agar sticks, just break each stick into pieces and grind them into fine flakes in a food processor. Powdered agar can be substituted for flakes at a ratio of about 1 teaspoon powder to 1 tablespoon of flakes. The gelling ability of agar is affected by the acidity or alkalinity of the ingredients with which it is mixed. More acidic foods, such as citrus fruits, may require higher amounts of agar to gel properly. Store at room temperature in an airtight, moisture-proof container.

• **Arrowroot:** Arrowroot is a white, powdery, thickening agent ground more finely than flour. It is preferable to cornstarch because it provides a clear finish, rather than a cloudy paste. Arrowroot is extracted from rhizomes and was tradi-tionally used by American Indians to heal arrow wounds, hence the name. Arrowroot is less refined than cornstarch and thickens at lower temperatures than either flour or cornstarch. It must first be combined with a cool liquid or water before using. Replace cornstarch with arrowroot measure for measure in recipes. Look for it at your natural food store, and keep it at room temperature in an air-tight, moisture-proof container.

• **Balsamic vinegar:** Balsamic vinegar is dark brown with an exquisite fla-vor and subtle sweetness. It is made from sweet Trebbiano grapes and acquires its dark color and pungency from being aged in wooden barrels for a minimum of ten years. Balsamic vinegar is available in supermarkets, Italian grocery stores, and gourmet and specialty food shops.

• **Brown rice syrup:** This is a delicate, mild sweetener. It is made from sprouted sweet rice that has been dried, ground, and then heated with water and cooked into a syrup. Store it at room temperature or in the refrigerator in warm weather to prevent mold. Brown rice syrup can be found at natural food stores.

• **Brown rice vinegar:** This delicately flavored, amber-colored vinegar is made from either fermented brown rice or unrefined rice wine. It is available in natural food stores and some supermarkets. Beware of most grocery store "seasoned" rice vinegars, as these typically contain added sugar. Stored at room temperature, brown rice vinegar will keep indefinitely.

• **Chickpea flour:** This versatile, delicious, gluten-free flour also is known as *besan, gram flour, cici flour, chana flour*, and *garbanzo bean flour*. It is tan in color because it is made from ground chickpeas. Chickpea flour is commonly used in Indian, Italian, and some Middle Eastern cuisines. Look for it in Indian markets and natural food stores.

• **Kuzu:** This thickener is made from the tuber of the kudzu plant. Also known as kudzu starch, it is used as a thickening agent similar to cornstarch, arrowroot, or potato starch. There are a number of characteristics of kuzu that distinguish it from other starches: kuzu starch creates a smooth, creamy consistency and a clear shine in jelled foods; its mild flavor does not conflict with delicate or subtle flavors; it produces a crispy texture when the powder is dusted over foods prior to deep frying; and its alkalinity allows the starch to harmonize well with sugars, which are acidic. Kuzu comes in small chunks. To measure, crush the chunks into a powder. To thicken a liquid, mix the powder with an equal amount of cold water, then stir the mixture into the hot liquid and simmer for a few minutes until the sauce is thickened. Look for kuzu in your natural food store.

• **Miso:** Miso is a salty, flavorful, fermented soybean paste that often contains rice, barley, or another grain or bean. Some specialty misos are made from chickpeas, lentils, adzuki beans, or other legumes instead of soybeans. Used primarily as a seasoning, miso's characteristics range from dark and strongly flavored to light, smooth, and delicately flavored. The best varieties will be found in the refrigerated section of your natural food store, as they retain active enzymes. Store miso in a tightly covered container in the refrigerator where it will keep for several months to a year (check the "use by" date on the container).

Note: If you are unable to have soy products, always use chickpea miso in recipes that otherwise are soy free.

• **Nondairy milk:** Nondairy milk refers to any creamy, plant-based beverage such as soy, rice, oat, almond, or mixed grain beverages. Look for them in aseptic boxes on the shelf at your natural food store or in cartons in the dairy case.

Because nondairy milks come in a variety of flavors (such as vanilla, chocolate, and carob), always looks for "plain" unflavored nondairy milk when making uncheeses and other savory dishes. Opened nondairy milk should be stored in the refrigerator. It will keep for about seven to ten days.

• **Nutritional yeast:** See page 32.

• **Sesame tahini:** Sesame tahini is a smooth, creamy, tan-colored paste made from finely ground raw or roasted sesame seeds. It is an essential ingredient in many Middle Eastern recipes and adds a wonderful texture and nutty flavor to spreads, sauces, and dressings. Tahini may be very thick, like peanut butter, or thin and slightly runny depending on the brand. As with all unrefined nut and seed butters, you'll want to store tahini in the refrigerator to keep it from becoming rancid and to keep the oil from separating. However, if the oil does separate, simply stir it back in. Sesame tahini is available in many supermarkets, Middle Eastern grocery stores, and natural food stores.

• **Tamari:** Typical grocery store brands of "soy sauce" are little more than hydrolyzed vegetable protein, sugar, and caramel coloring. However, excellent, naturally fermented soy sauce, commonly called *tamari*, is readily available in natural food stores and some supermarkets. As you'll see on its label, it contains only soybeans, salt, water, and sometimes wheat. Good soy sauces with reduced sodium also are available. If you have a sensitivity to yeast or fermented foods, look for Bragg Liquid Aminos, a rich, savory soy product that has not been fermented. You can substitute it equally for tamari.

• **Toasted sesame oil:** This oil is extracted from toasted sesame seeds and has a luscious, highly concentrated flavor. A few drops sprinkled over cooked grains, beans, pasta, or vegetables add outstanding flavor, especially when combined with a little tamari soy sauce. It also comes in a spicy hot pepper variety. Do not use toasted sesame oil for cooking or sautéing, as it burns easily. You'll find it in your natural food store. Be sure to refrigerate it after opening.

• **Tofu:** Tofu, also known as soybean curd, is a soft, cheese-like food made by curdling fresh hot soymilk with a coagulant. Traditionally the curdling agent is nigari, a compound found in natural ocean water, or calcium sulfate, a naturally occurring mineral. Curds also can be produced by adding acidic foods, such as lemon juice or vinegar. The curds are then pressed into a solid block.

Tofu is rich in high-quality protein. It also is a good source of B-vitamins and iron. When the curdling agent used to make tofu is calcium salt, the tofu is an excellent source of calcium. Generally, the softer the tofu, the lower the fat content. Tofu is very low in sodium, making it a perfect food for people on sodium-restricted diets. In recipes, tofu has the uncanny ability to take on any flavorings that are added to it. Three main types of tofu are available in stores throughout North America:

Firm regular tofu (also called Chinese tofu or water-packed tofu) is sold in a sealed tub or box. It holds up well in stir-fry dishes, soups, or on the grill—anywhere that you want it to maintain its shape. Firm regular tofu generally is higher in protein, fat, and calcium than other types.

Soft regular tofu is a good choice for recipes that call for blended tofu or for use in Asian-style dishes.

Silken tofu (also called Japanese tofu) is made using a slightly different process that results in a creamy, custard-like product. Silken tofu works well in pureed or blended dishes, such as smoothies, puddings, and creamy soups. It comes in variety of firmnesses ranging from soft to extra firm.

Tofu is sold in water-filled tubs, vacuum packs, or in aseptic brick packages. You'll find it in the produce section of grocery stores, although some stores keep it in the dairy or deli sections. Sometimes it is sold in bulk in food cooperatives or Asian markets. Unless it is aseptically packaged, it should be kept cold. As with any perishable food, check the expiration date on the package.

Once the package is open, leftover tofu should be rinsed and covered with fresh water for storage. Change the water daily to keep it fresh, and use it within a week.

• **Umeboshi plum paste:** Umeboshi plums are a variety of apricot that is pickled in salt and an herb called red shiso leaf. They are used as a condiment in Japanese and macrobiotic cuisine. The paste and vinegar have a salty, tart flavor and make delightful seasonings. When using umeboshi, avoid adding salt to your recipe. Umeboshi paste should be stored in a sealed container in the refrigerator; it will keep for several months. The vinegar can be kept at room temperature. Look for umeboshi plum paste in the macrobiotic section of your natural food store. The vinegar can be found in the condiment aisle.

ABOUT THE NUTRITIONAL ANALYSES AND RECIPE PREPARATION

Dairy cheese, by its very nature, is high in animal fat, cholesterol, milk protein (casein), lactose, calories, and sodium. The recipes in *The Ultimate Uncheese Cookbook* replicate all that is best loved about cheese while striving to eliminate most of its shortcomings. For your convenience, nutritional breakdowns and suggested serving sizes accompany each recipe.

The calculations for the nutritional analyses are based on the average number of servings per recipe and the average amount of an ingredient if a range is provided. Calculations are rounded up to the nearest gram. If two options for an ingredient are listed, the first one is analyzed. Not included are optional ingredients, serving suggestions, or fat used for frying, unless the amount of fat is specified in the recipe.

At first glance, uncheeses may appear to be moderately high in fat. Keep in mind that nondairy "cheese" products, akin to their dairy counterparts, are intended to be consumed as condiments. That is, they should add flavor and substance to dishes but not be the dish itself. When you round out your meals with fat-free fruits, vegetables, legumes, and whole grains, your overall fat intake will remain within healthful bounds, even with the inclusion of these delicious, nondairy uncheeses.

Any fat in the recipes comes solely from vegetable sources. There are no animal-based fats to add cholesterol to your diet, no hydrogenated or saturated fats, no synthetic fat substitutes or chemical flavor enhancers, and no artificial colors. By reducing or eliminating your consumption of animal products and keeping high-fat plant foods (such as nuts, avocados, coconut, and olives) to a minimum, you will ensure your diet is within the healthiest recommendations.

If you would like to reduce or remove the fat in any recipe that contains less than $1/2$ cup of nuts, nut butter, or sesame tahini, feel free to halve the amount called for or eliminate it completely. This will not affect the appearance of the dish, although it will produce a somewhat less rich and cheesy taste. If you substitute fat-reduced tofu for the full-fat variety, you can reduce the fat to almost nil in recipes calling for tofu

Salt is a flavor most often associated with cheese. If any uncheese recipe seems too highly seasoned with salty ingredients for your taste, simply reduce the amount called for by up to half, or if you prefer, exclude it altogether. If you like, you can enhance the sharpness of the recipe by increasing the amount of lemon juice or vinegar or adding a pinch of citric acid powder. On the other hand, if you prefer a less sharp taste, simply reduce these acidic ingredients. Feel free to fine-tune any other seasonings as well. If you prefer more or less garlic, mustard, or hot seasonings, go right ahead and make the adjustments you want. Modifying the seasonings will not affect the outcome of the recipe other than make it more to your satisfaction.

It is best, at least initially, to prepare each recipe as directed. Once you know how it was intended to turn out and are confident with the preparation techniques, go ahead and experiment. One of the unique joys of uncheesing is that most recipes can be easily adapted to suit individual preferences.

There are countless reasons why more and more people are doing away with dairy products. Whatever your motivation, I hope the recipes in *The Ultimate Uncheese Cookbook* will allow you to "have your cheese and eat it, too!"

GETTING THAT CHEESY TASTE

As a source of calories, fat, and cholesterol, cheese can't be beat. Slabs of cheese weigh down grocery checkout scales everywhere. Unfortunately, bathroom scales reflect a similar trend. Fortunately, breaking free of cheese is easy, and the results–on the scale, on your cholesterol levels, and in how you feel every day–can be spectacular.

In addition to the recipes in this book, here are some easy kitchen tricks that will make it a breeze to get that cheesy taste:

• Avocado can substitute for the rich and creamy "mouth feel" of cheese on sandwiches, salads, or in Mexican food. It is much lower in saturated fat than cheese, and most of the remaining fat content is monounsaturated.

• Nutritional yeast is an extremely versatile topping that lends a cheesy flavor to spaghetti sauce, stews, casseroles, and even pizza. Because it is an inactive yeast, it doesn't have any leavening power, as does yeast used for bread baking. Instead, it is prized for its delicious "cheesy" taste and high nutritional content. When mixed with certain seasonings, nutritional yeast also can impart a poultry-like flavor. Nutritional yeast is a concentrated source of protein and a good source of many B-complex vitamins. A serving of $1^1/_2$ heaping tablespoons (16g) has only 47 calories, boasts 8 grams of protein, and contains only 0.8 grams of fat.

Pure nutritional yeast (Red Star Vegetarian Support Formula) is most commonly found in the bulk section of natural food stores. Also look for the Red Star repack Kal Vegetarian Support Formula nutritional yeast in the bright yellow canister on your natural grocer's shelf. A serving (about $1^1/_2$ to 2 tablespoons) of Vegetarian Support Formula flakes contains a full-day's supply of vitamin B_{12}. Some brands of packaged nutritional yeast have been combined with whey, a byproduct of cheese processing, so be sure to read package labels. Vegetarian Support Formula nutritional yeast also may be ordered in bulk from The Mail Order Catalog, Box 180, Summertown, TN 38483. Call for current price information at 1-800-695-2241 or visit their Web site at www.healthy-eating.com.

Do not confuse nutritional yeast with brewer's yeast. Nutritional yeast is a primary grown food crop with a delicious taste. Brewer's yeast is a byproduct of the brewing industry and is extremely bitter. Nutritional yeast is available in flakes or powder, but you'll probably find the flakes more versatile and delicious. If you only have access to powdered nutritional yeast (that is, nutritional yeast that is finely ground with no visible flakes), use a scant $1^1/_2$ tablespoons of powder for each 2 tablespoons of flakes called for in a recipe.

• Top casseroles and pasta with ground nuts or seeds instead of cheese.

• Stir sesame tahini or cashew butter into soups, sauces, gravies, or spreads for added richness and a creamy texture.

• Add small amounts of light miso or soy sauce to provide the saltiness of cheese in recipes and add a rich, aged flavor.

UNCHEESE SPREADS, DIPS, PESTOS, AND SPRINKLES

If you are a cheese lover, the recipes in this section will knock your socks off. They are about as close as you can get to "the real thing" without dairy. Even better, they are made with whole, natural ingredients, so you can rejoice guilt-free as you savor every bite. Use these remarkable creations just as you would use any comparable cheese-based food—as a snack; at a wine tasting; as a sandwich filling; as a topping for pasta; as a dip for chips, pretzels, crackers, and flat bread; or as an ingredients in soups, sauces, and casseroles. If you miss cheese, your wishes have been answered. Dive into these recipes and let your imagination run wild—you are about to experience the ultimate in uncheese ecstasy!

MAKES 1¼ CUPS

This French-inspired garlic, black pepper, and herb uncheese is marvelous on bread or crackers and equally scrumptious piled on baked or steamed potatoes. Use it as a condiment scooped on top of pasta along with your favorite tomato-based sauce.

Per 2 tablespoons:	
calories	60
protein	3 g
fat	2 g
carbohydrate	7 g
calcium	26 mg
sodium	50 mg

FREE OF:
GLUTEN
SOY
NUTS
YEAST
CORN

Contains umeboshi plum paste.

White Bean Boursin

2 cups drained cooked or canned white beans (one 15- or 16-ounce can)

2 tablespoons extra-virgin olive oil

1 tablespoon umeboshi plum paste

1 teaspoon dried basil

1 teaspoon dried marjoram

½ teaspoon dried thyme

2 cloves roasted garlic, or ½ teaspoon crushed fresh garlic

¼ teaspoon pepper, or more to taste

⅛ teaspoon ground rosemary

Place all ingredients in a food processor and blend into a very thick, smooth paste, stopping to scrape down the sides of the work bowl as necessary. Chill several hours or overnight before serving to allow flavors to blend. Keeps 5 to 7 days in the refrigerator.

Tofu Boursin

Omit beans and olive oil. Drain ½ pound (8 ounces) firm regular tofu and break into large chunks. Place in a saucepan and cover with water. Bring to a boil, reduce heat, and simmer 5 minutes. Drain well. Chill uncovered in the refrigerator until cool enough to handle. Crumble and place in a food processor with ¼ cup vegan mayonnaise and remaining ingredients. Proceed with directions above.

Creamy Onion–Cheez Spread

Omit herbs (basil, marjoram, thyme, and rosemary) and pepper. Add 2 tablespoons vegan dry onion soup mix during processing.

White Bean Liptauer

MAKES 1⅔ CUPS

2 cups drained cooked or canned white beans
(one 15- or 16-ounce can)

2 tablespoons extra-virgin olive oil

1 tablespoon drained capers

1 tablespoon chopped scallions or chives, or more to taste

2 teaspoons umeboshi plum paste

2 teaspoons ground caraway seeds

1 teaspoon dry mustard

Paprika

This nondairy version of the classic Hungarian cheese appetizer is both savory and distinctive. Serve it as a dip for vegetables or as a spread for sandwiches or crackers.

Place all ingredients except paprika in a food processor and process several minutes into a smooth paste, stopping to scrape down sides of work bowl as necessary. Chill several hours or overnight before serving to allow flavors to blend. To serve, form mixture into a mound and sprinkle liberally with paprika to thoroughly cover top and sides. Keeps 5 to 7 days in the refrigerator.

Variation

• Instead of forming into a mound, use as a spread for bread. Once spread, sprinkle the top generously with paprika.

Liptauer Käse

Omit beans and olive oil. Drain ½ pound (8 ounces) firm regular tofu and break into large chunks. Place in a saucepan and cover with water. Bring to a boil, reduce heat, and simmer 5 minutes. Drain well. Chill uncovered in the refrigerator until cool enough to handle. Crumble and place in a food processor with ⅓ cup vegan mayonnaise and remaining ingredients except paprika. Proceed with directions above.

FREE OF: GLUTEN SOY NUTS YEAST CORN

Per 2 tablespoons:

calories	59
protein	3 g
fat	2 g
carbohydrate	7 g
calcium	26 mg
sodium	66 mg

Contains capers and umeboshi plum paste.

Crock Cheez

This cheddar-style spread is sharp, tangy, and rich. It is reminiscent of the grainy, aged spreads found in small, brown pottery crocks in gourmet restaurants and specialty food shops.

½ pound (8 ounces) firm regular tofu, drained

3 tablespoons nutritional yeast flakes

2 tablespoons sesame tahini or raw cashew butter

2 tablespoons fresh lemon juice

1½ tablespoons light or chickpea miso

1 teaspoon onion powder

¾ teaspoon salt

½ teaspoon paprika

¼ teaspoon garlic powder

¼ teaspoon dry mustard

Break tofu into large chunks. Place in a saucepan and cover with water. Bring to a boil, reduce heat, and simmer 5 minutes. Drain well. Chill uncovered in the refrigerator until cool enough to handle. Crumble and place in a food processor with remaining ingredients. Process into a smooth paste, stopping to scrape down sides of work bowl as necessary. Chill several hours or overnight before serving to allow flavors to blend. Keeps 5 to 7 days in the refrigerator.

Per 2 tablespoons:	
calories	53
protein	5 g
fat	3 g
carbohydrate	7 g
calcium	26 mg
sodium	66 mg

FREE OF:
GLUTEN
NUTS
CORN

Contains sesame tahini.

Derby Sage Cheez

Add 1 teaspoon dried sage prior to processing.

Fiery Crock Cheez

Add ⅛ teaspoon cayenne, or more to taste, prior to processing.

Horseradish Crock Cheez

Add 1 tablespoon prepared white horseradish (not creamed) prior to processing.

Smoked Crock Cheez

Add ¼ teaspoon liquid hickory smoke prior to processing.

Bugsy's Crock Cheez

Stir into mixture ⅓ cup finely grated carrot, 3 tablespoons minced scallions, and 2 tablespoons minced fresh parsley after processing.

Crock Cheez Gone Meshuga

Use all the variations listed above at once.

Plum Good Crock Cheez

Replace miso with an equal amount of umeboshi plum paste. Reduce salt to ¼ teaspoon or to taste.

MAKES ABOUT 2 CUPS

This tangy soy-free cheez is out of this world. Use it as a spread for bread or crackers, a dip for veggies, or a topping for grains, pizza, or potatoes. Stir it into sauces, gravies, soups, or casseroles whenever you want to add a spark of sharp, cheddary flavor.

Chick Cheez

2 cups drained cooked or canned chickpeas
   (one 15- or 16-ounce can)

3 tablespoons nutritional yeast flakes

2 tablespoons sesame tahini or raw cashew butter

2 tablespoons fresh lemon juice or white wine vinegar

1½ tablespoons light or chickpea miso

1 to 2 tablespoons extra-virgin olive oil

1 teaspoon onion powder

¾ teaspoon salt

½ teaspoon paprika

¼ teaspoon garlic powder

¼ teaspoon dry mustard

Combine all ingredients in a food processor fitted with a metal blade. Process into a smooth paste, stopping to scrape down sides of work bowl as necessary. Chill several hours or overnight before serving to allow flavors to blend. Keeps 5 to 7 days in the refrigerator.

White Bean Crock Cheez

Substitute 2 cups cooked white beans for the chickpeas.

Variations

• Use any of the variations for Crock Cheez, p. 36.

• For a delicious cheddary sauce, thin Crock Cheez, Chick Cheez, or White Bean Crock Cheez with a little plain nondairy milk or water until desired consistency is reached. Warm through over low heat. Serve over pasta, potatoes, grains, or vegetables.

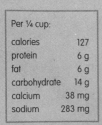

Per ¼ cup:	
calories	127
protein	6 g
fat	6 g
carbohydrate	14 g
calcium	38 mg
sodium	283 mg

FREE OF:
GLUTEN
SOY
NUTS
CORN

Contains sesame tahini.

Gee Whiz Spread

2 cups drained cooked or canned white beans
(one 15- or 16-ounce can)

½ cup roasted red peppers (skin and seeds removed),
or pimiento pieces

6 to 8 tablespoons nutritional yeast flakes

3 tablespoons fresh lemon juice

2 to 3 tablespoons sesame tahini or cashew butter

½ teaspoon prepared yellow mustard

½ teaspoon salt

¼ teaspoon each: garlic and onion powder

Place all ingredients in a food processor and process until completely smooth and evenly colored (this may take several minutes). Stop processor and scrape down sides of bowl as necessary during processing. Chill thoroughly before serving. Keeps 5 to 7 days in the refrigerator.

Variations

• In place of the red peppers, use ½ cup cooked chopped carrots, or ¾ teaspoon paprika, or 2 tablespoons unsalted tomato paste.

• For an "aged cheddar" flavor, add 1 to 2 teaspoons light or chickpea miso.

Have you ever longed for good, old-fashioned American cheese? Well, here is an all-American spread you can feel great about! Gee Whiz Spread is an amazing, versatile, whole food that is remarkably fast and simple to prepare. It's great on crackers and sandwiches or in almost any recipe that calls for dairy cheddar cheese. Spread it on buns for "cheez-burgers," or add a few spoonfuls to your favorite soup or sauce to turn them into cheezy delights.

FREE OF:
GLUTEN
SOY
NUTS
CORN

Per 2 tablespoons:	
calories	58
protein	4 g
fat	1 g
carbohydrate	8 g
calcium	28 mg
sodium	72 mg

Contains sesame tahini.

Tofu Pâté

MAKES 1½ CUPS
OR 3 CUPS

This quick and easy pâté is so impressively delicious that no one will guess it took mere minutes to make.

Small Batch		Large Batch
½ pound (8 ounces)	firm regular tofu, drained	1 pound (16 ounces)
2 tablespoons	sesame tahini	¼ cup
1 tablespoon	light or chickpea miso	2 tablespoons
2 teaspoons	tamari (or to taste)	1 tablespoon, plus 1 teaspoon
½ cup	shredded carrot	1 cup
¼ cup	sliced scallions	½ cup

Break tofu into large chunks. Place in a saucepan and cover with water. Bring to a boil, reduce heat, and simmer 5 minutes. Drain well. Chill uncovered in the refrigerator until cool enough to handle. Crumble and place in a food processor with tahini, miso, and tamari. Process into a smooth paste, stopping to scrape down sides of work bowl as necessary. Add carrot and scallions, and pulse until they are evenly distributed. Chill several hours or overnight before serving to allow flavors to blend. Keeps 5 to 7 days in the refrigerator.

Per 2 tablespoons:

calories	48
protein	4 g
fat	3 g
carbohydrate	3 g
calcium	52 mg
sodium	96 mg

FREE OF:
GLUTEN
NUTS
YEAST
CORN

Contains miso and tamari.

Cashew-Sesame Bean Cheez

A luscious combination of cashew butter and tahini contributes a rich, naturally sweet flavor reminiscent of dairy cream cheese.

2 cups drained cooked or canned white beans
   (one 15- or 16-ounce can)

1 cup fresh lemon juice

¾ cup cashew butter

⅓ cup sesame tahini

Salt

1 or 2 tablespoons water, if needed

Chop beans in a food processor fitted with a metal blade. Add remaining ingredients, using water only if needed to facilitate processing. Whip into a smooth, thick paste. Keeps 5 to 7 days in the refrigerator.

FREE OF: GLUTEN SOY YEAST CORN	Per 2 tablespoons:	
	calories	106
	protein	4 g
	fat	7 g
	carbohydrate	9 g
	calcium	37 mg
	sodium	5 mg

Port Wine Uncheese

With rich undertones of wine and cheddar, this plum-colored spread is sure to please.

2 cups drained cooked or canned pinto beans
   (one 15- or 16-ounce can)

¼ cup nonalcoholic red wine

3 tablespoons sesame tahini

1 tablespoon light or chickpea miso

Place all ingredients in a food processor and process until very smooth. Chill several hours before serving to allow flavors to blend. Keeps 5 to 7 days refrigerated.

FREE OF: GLUTEN SOY NUTS YEAST CORN	Per 2 tablespoons:	
	calories	67
	protein	3 g
	fat	2 g
	carbohydrate	9 g
	calcium	30 mg
	sodium	38 mg

Contains sesame tahini and red wine.

MAKES ABOUT 1 CUP

This amazing spread is thick, rich-tasting, and remarkably low in fat compared to dairy-based cream cheese. It is an ideal spread to top bagels, rice cakes, toast, or crackers.

Incredible Almond Creme Cheez

¼ cup blanched raw almonds (see Tip below)

½ cup hot water

½ cup cold water

2 tablespoons fresh lemon juice

2 tablespoons kuzu, arrowroot, or cornstarch

½ teaspoon nutritional yeast flakes

½ teaspoon salt

Grind the almonds to a fine powder in a food processor fitted with a metal blade or in an electric coffee grinder. Place in blender with ½ cup hot water and process to create a smooth, thick cream. Add ½ cup cold water and remaining ingredients. Blend on high until smooth and creamy.

Pour into 1-quart saucepan and bring to a boil, stirring constantly. After mixture thickens, reduce heat to medium and continue to cook, stirring constantly, 1 minute longer. Remove from heat and let cool.

Beat well with an electric beater, wire whisk, or fork. Transfer to storage container and chill in refrigerator. Creme Cheez will continue to thicken as it chills and will become very firm. It will keep in the refrigerator for about one week.

Important: Prior to serving, mash and beat again with an electric beater, wire whisk, or fork until smooth and creamy.

Tip: To blanch almonds, place in a saucepan with enough water to cover completely. Bring to a boil and simmer for 1 to 2 minutes. Drain and allow to cool, or rinse under cold water for rapid cooling. Pinch skins between thumb and forefinger at the base of each almond. Skins will slip off readily.

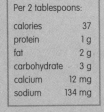

Per 2 tablespoons:

calories	37
protein	1 g
fat	2 g
carbohydrate	3 g
calcium	12 mg
sodium	134 mg

FREE OF:

GLUTEN
SOY
CORN

Herbed Creme Cheez

Stir 1 teaspoon dried parsley, ¼ teaspoon dried dillweed, ¼ teaspoon dried rosemary, ¼ teaspoon dried thyme, ¼ teaspoon crushed garlic, and ¼ teaspoon pepper into cooled mixture.

Pineapple Creme Cheez

Stir ¼ cup well-drained pineapple tidbits into cooled mixture.

Fruited Creme Cheez

Stir 1 to 2 tablespoons fruit-sweetened jam or preserves into cooled mixture.

Rich Tofu Creme Cheez

MAKES ABOUT 1⅔ CUPS

⅓ cup cashew butter

2 tablespoons fresh lemon juice

2 teaspoons mild sweet syrup (any kind; your choice)

1½ cups (about 12 ounces) crumbled firm silken tofu

1 teaspoon salt

Scant pinch of grated nutmeg

For scrumptious vegan "lox and cream cheese," top with strips of roasted red peppers.

Place all ingredients in a food processor and process until very smooth. Chill thoroughly before serving. Keeps 5 to 7 days in the refrigerator.

FREE OF:
GLUTEN
YEAST
CORN

Per 2 tablespoons:	
calories	61
protein	3 g
fat	4 g
carbohydrate	4 g
calcium	13 mg
sodium	176 mg

MAKES ABOUT ⅔ CUP

This spunky yet simple walnut-based pesto has astounding flavor. You can choose from fresh sweet basil, piquant cilantro, or pungent arugula, whichever you prefer. It's unbeatable!

Besto Pesto

1 cup firmly packed fresh basil, cilantro,
    or arugula (stems removed)
⅓ cup walnuts
¼ cup extra-virgin olive oil
1½ tablespoons light or chickpea miso
½ teaspoon crushed garlic
¼ teaspoon salt
1 tablespoon water, if needed

Combine all ingredients in a food processor fitted with a metal blade. Process until smooth, adding water only if needed to facilitate processing. Spoon the pesto liberally over pasta, potatoes, or rice, or just spread it on a slice of bread or toast. Best served immediately.

Per 2 tablespoons:	
calories	155
protein	2 g
fat	16 g
carbohydrate	3 g
calcium	15 mg
sodium	231 mg

FREE OF:
GLUTEN
SOY
YEAST
CORN

Contains miso.

Betta Feta

MAKES 2 CUPS (DRAINED)

1 pound (16 ounces) firm regular tofu,
   cut into ½-inch cubes

1½ cups water

½ cup light or chickpea miso

3 tablespoons white wine vinegar

2 teaspoons salt

This delicious faux feta tastes very much like dairy feta and is just as adaptable. Crumble it over pasta, grains, or raw vegetable salads.

Place tofu cubes in a medium saucepan and cover with water. Bring to a boil, reduce heat, cover and simmer 5 minutes. Drain well. While tofu is simmering, prepare brine by whisking together remaining ingredients. Add drained hot tofu cubes to brine and let cool at room temperature 20 minutes. Chill uncovered in refrigerator until cold to the touch. Cover and chill at least 2 to 7 days before serving. (The longer marinating time will produce a richer tasting, more flavorful feta.) Shake or stir contents occasionally to ensure all cubes are evenly covered with brine. Keeps at least 2 weeks in the refrigerator. To serve, remove feta with a slotted spoon and drain well.

FREE OF:
GLUTEN
NUTS
YEAST
CORN

Per ¼ cup:	
calories	61
protein	6 g
fat	3 g
carbohydrate	4 g
calcium	60 mg

Contains vinegar and miso.

Use this versatile nondairy mixture in any traditional recipe that calls for creamy ricotta cheese. Omit the optional seasonings for use in sweeter fare and dessert recipes.

Per ¼ cup:	
calories	78
protein	8 g
fat	4 g
carbohydrate	4 g
calcium	105 mg

FREE OF:
GLUTEN
NUTS
YEAST
CORN

This is an excellent replacement for dairy cottage cheese.

Per ½ cup:	
calories	144
protein	10 g
fat	10 g
carbohydrate	3 g
calcium	133 mg
sodium	478 mg

FREE OF:
GLUTEN
NUTS
YEAST
CORN

Tofu Ricotta

1 pound (16 ounces) firm regular tofu, drained

3 tablespoons fresh lemon juice

2 teaspoons mild sweet syrup (your choice)

1 teaspoon dried basil (optional)

½ teaspoon salt

¼ teaspoon garlic powder (optional)

Break tofu into large chunks. Place in a saucepan and cover with water. Bring to a boil, reduce heat, and simmer for 5 minutes. Drain well. Chill uncovered in the refrigerator until cool enough to handle. Crumble and place in a bowl with remaining ingredients. Mash and blend until mixture has a fine, grainy texture similar to ricotta or cottage cheese. Chill several hours or overnight before serving to allow flavors to blend. Will keep in refrigerator for about 5 days.

Creamy Cottage Cheez

1 pound (16 ounces) firm regular tofu, drained

⅔ cup vegan mayonnaise

2 teaspoons onion powder (optional)

1 teaspoon garlic powder (optional)

1 teaspoon salt

1 teaspoon dried dillweed, ground dill seed, or ground caraway seed (optional)

Follow directions above for Tofu Ricotta.

Spicy Herb and Tomato Cheez Spread

Enjoy this thick, savory, colorful spread on bread or crackers or as a vegetable dip. It also makes a sophisticated filling for grilled cheez sandwiches or a tantalizing spread for cheezy veggie burgers.

½ cup nutritional yeast flakes

¼ cup oat flour or chickpea flour

1 cup water

2 tablespoons ketchup

1 tablespoon olive oil

1 teaspoon onion powder

½ teaspoon garlic powder

¼ teaspoon salt

¼ teaspoon dried thyme

¼ teaspoon paprika

⅛ teaspoon pepper

Pinch of cayenne

Place the nutritional yeast flakes and flour in a medium bowl. Gradually whisk in the water, taking care to avoid lumps. Whisk in remaining ingredients until smooth. Pour into a small saucepan and cook over medium heat, stirring or whisking constantly until very thick and smooth. Serve hot, warm, or thoroughly chilled. Keeps about 5 to 7 days in the refrigerator.

FREE OF:
GLUTEN
SOY
NUTS
CORN

Per ¼ cup:	
calories	110
protein	10 g
fat	5 g
carbohydrate	12 g
calcium	15 mg
sodium	227 mg

MAKES 2 CUPS

High in fiber as well as flavor, this zippy cheez spread is great for sandwiches and snacks. If you use canned beans, it's a snap to prepare.

Chickpea Havarti Spread

1 cup water

2 cups drained cooked or canned chickpeas
    (one 15- or 16-ounce can)

½ cup raw cashews

⅓ cup nutritional yeast flakes

2 teaspoons onion powder

1 teaspoon salt

½ teaspoon garlic powder

½ teaspoon ground dill seed

½ teaspoon whole celery seed

¼ cup fresh lemon juice

Place all ingredients in a blender and process until smooth. Pour into a medium saucepan and cook and stir over moderate heat until very thick, about 15 to 20 minutes. Remove from heat and cool, cover, and chill for several hours or overnight before serving. Keeps 5 to 7 days in the refrigerator.

Per ¼ cup:

calories	138
protein	8 g
fat	6 g
carbohydrate	17 g
calcium	28 mg
sodium	272 mg

FREE OF:
GLUTEN
SOY
CORN

Hot Parmesan Artichoke Dip

2 (14-ounce) cans artichoke hearts, drained well and quartered

1½ cups (12 ounces) crumbled firm silken tofu, or 1 cup drained cooked or canned white beans

½ cup plain nondairy milk or water

2 teaspoons kuzu, arrowroot, or cornstarch

1 teaspoon dried basil

1 teaspoon dried oregano

1 teaspoon dried marjoram

¼ to ½ teaspoon crushed garlic

½ teaspoon salt

1 cup Parmezano Sprinkles (page 50) or vegan soy-based parmesan alternative

Preheat oven to 350°F. Place all ingredients, except Parmezano Sprinkles, in a blender or food processor and process until very smooth. Pour into a bowl and stir in the Parmezano Sprinkles. Transfer to a large, lightly oiled pie plate, quiche pan, or shallow casserole dish, and bake until lightly crusty on top (about 45 to 60 minutes, depending on the size of the baking dish). Serve hot, straight from the baking dish.

Hot Spinach–Artichoke Dip

Stir in 1 package frozen chopped spinach, thawed and squeezed to remove excess moisture, along with the vegan Parmezano Sprinkles.

Guests always appreciate this delicious hot appetizer that makes a scrumptious dip for vegetable sticks, pita triangles, or chips. It's also wonderful on sourdough or Italian bread. Try spreading it on toasted, whole-grain bread slices or English muffins, then broil for a few minutes until lightly browned and crusty. For best results, use either water-packed or seasoned, oil-packed artichoke hearts.

FREE OF:
GLUTEN
SOY
NUTS
CORN

Per 2 tablespoons:	
calories	32
protein	3 g
fat	1 g
carbohydrate	3 g
calcium	31 mg
sodium	175 mg

49

MAKES ABOUT 1 CUP

Sprinkle this delightful topping over pasta or pizza or wherever you would normally use Parmesan cheese. It is very easy to make if you have a food processor and costs less than commercial vegan Parmesan substitutes. Almonds and white sesame seeds will make the most authentic looking Parmezano, but if you are willing to expand your horizons try raw pumpkin seeds, roasted pistachios, walnuts, pignolia nuts, sunflower seeds, or any other nut or seed of your choice.

Parmezano Sprinkles

½ cup blanched almonds (see Tip on page 42), or white sesame seeds

2 tablespoons nutritional yeast flakes

1 to 2 teaspoons light or chickpea miso

Heaping ¼ teaspoon salt

Grind almonds or sesame seeds to a fine powder in a food processor fitted with a metal blade. Add remaining ingredients and pulse or process until well incorporated. Store in an airtight container in the refrigerator. Shake container before using to break up any lumps. Will keep for a month or longer in the refrigerator. May be frozen.

Tips: This recipe is easily doubled, tripled, or quadrupled, which can be very convenient, especially if you use it often.

• Blanched almonds may be ground in a food processor using a metal blade. You may find that sesame seeds are too small to be ground effectively in a food processor, or you may find they must be processed for a much longer time. If necessary or if you prefer, grind them in an electric coffee grinder or spice mill and then transfer the powder to a food processor.

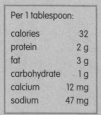

Per 1 tablespoon:		FREE OF:
calories	32	GLUTEN
protein	2 g	SOY
fat	3 g	NUTS
carbohydrate	1 g	CORN
calcium	12 mg	
sodium	47 mg	

For a nut-free version, use white sesame seeds.

Roasted Red Pepper and Garlic Spread

MAKES ABOUT 1¾ CUPS

2 (12-ounce) jars roasted red peppers, drained
  (skin and seeds removed)

½ cup Parmezano Sprinkles, page 50, or vegan
  soy-based parmesan alternative

¼ cup extra-virgin olive oil

1 teaspoon crushed fresh or roasted garlic

Salt and pepper

Combine all ingredients in a food processor and blend into a smooth purée. Store leftovers in refrigerator.

This exquisite spread is as delicious as it is beautiful. Slather it on warm, split and toasted French bread or toasted Italian bread, or toss it with your favorite pasta, and enjoy a slice of paradise.

FREE OF: GLUTEN SOY NUTS CORN	Per 2 tablespoons:	
	calories	66
	protein	1 g
	fat	5 g
	carbohydrate	4 g
	calcium	12 mg
	sodium	28 mg

Sofcheez Crumble

MAKES ABOUT 1 CUP

½ pound (8 ounces) firm regular tofu, rinsed and drained

1 tablespoon light or chickpea miso

2 teaspoons fresh lemon juice

¼ teaspoon salt

Crumble the tofu into a bowl. Add remaining ingredients and mash together with a fork.

Tip: To use in recipes that will not be cooked, slice or cube the tofu and place in a saucepan. Cover with water and bring to a boil. Reduce the heat and simmer for 5 minutes. Drain well. Chill uncovered in the refrigerator until cool enough to handle. Crumble and mash with other ingredients. Chill several hours before using.

This is reminiscent of fresh goat's milk cheese. Use it as a topping for pizza, lasagne, casseroles, or other foods that will be cooked.

FREE OF: GLUTEN NUTS YEAST CORN	Per 2 tablespoons:	
	calories	46
	protein	5 g
	fat	3 g
	carbohydrate	2 g
	calcium	58 mg
	sodium	122 mg

Contains miso.

MAKES 1¼ CUPS

This is an excellent all-purpose seasoning for sauces, gravies, potatoes, grains, and vegetables. It even makes an instant soup broth (see Tip).

All-Season Blend

1½ cups nutritional yeast flakes

3 tablespoons salt

1 tablespoon onion powder

1 tablespoon paprika

2 teaspoons garlic powder

1 teaspoon dried parsley flakes

½ teaspoon turmeric

¼ teaspoon dried thyme

¼ teaspoon dried marjoram

¼ teaspoon dried dillweed

¼ teaspoon pepper

Combine all ingredients in a blender or food processor and process until finely ground and powdery. Store in an airtight container at room temperature.

Tip: For Instant Veggie Broth, combine 1½ teaspoons All-Season Blend with 1 cup water in a small saucepan. Bring to a boil, simmer 1 minute, and serve. Quantities are easily doubled, tripled, or quadrupled.

Per 1 teaspoon:	
calories	9
protein	2 g
fat	0 g
carbohydrate	1 g
calcium	2 mg
sodium	321 mg

FREE OF:
GLUTEN
SOY
NUTS
CORN

CHEEZY HOT AND
COLD SAUCES

If you miss that cheese flavor, you'll find these cheesy-tasting sauces to be ideal for satisfying your cravings. Most of the recipes in this section can be made in a flash, so there's not a lot of waiting involved when those "cheese urges" strike. They are superb over biscuits, bread, toast, pizza, English muffins, nacho chips, baked or steamed potatoes, quinoa, couscous, all types of rice or pasta, and every vegetable imaginable. The consistency ranges from thick and luscious to thin and saucy, so you can be creative with how you use them. While cheez sauces are best served with other foods, they are so scrumptious you might be tempted to eat them straight out of the pot with a spoon!

Special Notes:

• If you are unable to have gluten, always use a gluten-free flour (such as chickpea or rice flour) with any recipe in this section that calls for flour. Gluten-free options will not affect the outcome of the sauces.

• Leftover sauces should be stored in the refrigerator. They will become very thick and firm when chilled but will turn "melty" again when gently reheated. Very low heat or a double boiler works well for reheating. Thin the sauces with a little water or plain nondairy milk, if desired.

MAKES 4 TO 5 CUPS

I've often fantasized about a sauce as velvety smooth and cheezy as the one I imagine June Cleaver made for Ward, Wally, and The Beaver. But mine, of course, would be dairy-free and low enough in fat so I could indulge with pleasure. If you are like me, wait no longer! Here is an all-American cheez sauce that is rich-tasting, soothing, and satisfying. Pour it over broccoli, potatoes, or macaroni to instantly create those Norman Rockwell dishes. For an extraordinary fondue, serve this sauce from a fondue pot accompanied by all your dipping favorites: bread cubes, vegetables, or even chunks of fresh fruit.

Per ½ cup:	
calories	84
protein	9 g
fat	2 g
carbohydrate	12 g
calcium	25 mg
sodium	227 mg

FREE OF:
GLUTEN
SOY
NUTS
CORN

Unprocessed Cheez Sauce

1 medium potato, peeled and coarsely chopped

1 or 2 medium carrots, coarsely chopped

1 medium onion, coarsely chopped

1 cup water

½ to 1 cup crumbled firm silken tofu, or ½ to 1 cup cooked and drained white beans

½ to 1 cup nutritional yeast flakes

2 to 4 tablespoons miso (dark, light, or chickpea)

1 to 2 tablespoons fresh lemon juice

1¼ teaspoons salt, or to taste

2 teaspoons garlic powder

Combine potato, carrot, onion, and water in a medium saucepan and bring to a boil. Cover and reduce heat to medium. Simmer until vegetables are tender, about 10 minutes. Transfer to a blender along with remaining ingredients. Process until velvety smooth. Serve immediately or return to saucepan or fondue pot to keep warm.

Tips: If mixture fills your blender more than halfway, blend in two or three batches.

• The larger quantities of tofu or beans and nutritional yeast will make a thicker, richer-tasting sauce.

Chick-E-Cheez Sauce

⅔ cup nutritional yeast flakes

½ cup chickpea flour

2 cups water

2 tablespoons olive oil or organic canola or safflower oil

¾ teaspoon salt

½ teaspoon dried thyme, basil, oregano, or dillweed (optional)

½ teaspoon onion powder

½ teaspoon garlic powder

⅛ teaspoon pepper (optional)

1 to 2 tablespoons light or chickpea miso (optional)

2 to 3 teaspoons fresh lemon juice

This is a versatile cheez sauce that is quick and easy to make. Season it with your favorite dried herbs and pour it over pasta or potatoes combined with steamed vegetables for a "fast food" dinner the whole family will enjoy. This sauce also makes a delicious fondue.

Place the yeast flakes and flour in a medium bowl. Gradually whisk in the water, taking care to avoid lumps. Whisk in remaining ingredients except miso, if using, and lemon juice until smooth. Pour into a medium saucepan and cook over medium heat, stirring or whisking almost constantly until very thick and smooth. Remove from heat and whip in miso and lemon juice to taste. Serve hot, warm, or thoroughly chilled. Keeps about 5 to 7 days in the refrigerator.

Tip: If you prefer, whole wheat flour or any other flour of your choice may be substituted for the chickpea flour.

FREE OF:
GLUTEN
SOY
NUTS
CORN

Per ½ cup:

calories	165
protein	14 g
fat	10 g
carbohydrate	11 g
calcium	34 mg
sodium	407 mg

Create instant Alfredo noodles or au gratin dishes with this rich and remarkable dairy-free sauce. It's also great served chilled over salads or fresh tomato wedges.

Cashew Cheez Sauce

½ cup cashew butter

3 tablespoons fresh lemon juice

3 tablespoons nutritional yeast flakes

1½ tablespoons light or chickpea miso

1 teaspoon onion powder

Pinch of garlic powder

1 cup water, more or less as needed

Salt

Place all ingredients in a blender or food processor and process until very smooth and creamy. Use just enough water to make a thick but pourable sauce. Alternatively, combine cashew butter, lemon juice, nutritional yeast, miso, and powders in a bowl. Mix until smooth. Gradually beat in water using a wire whisk. Serve chilled, at room temperature, or warm. To serve warm, heat over low, stirring almost constantly. Do not boil. Add more water if sauce becomes too thick.

Smoky Cashew Cheez Sauce

Add a few drops liquid hickory smoke to taste.

Per ½ cup:	
calories	221
protein	10 g
fat	17 g
carbohydrate	14 g
calcium	18 mg
sodium	160 mg

FREE OF:
GLUTEN
SOY
CORN

Cashew Sour Cream Sauce

½ cup cashew butter

2 tablespoons fresh lemon juice

Salt

1 cup hot or cold water, more or less as needed

Combine all ingredients in a blender or food processor, using just enough water to make a thick, smooth sauce. Alternatively, combine all ingredients, except water, in small bowl. Gradually stir in enough water to make a thick but pourable sauce.

Salsa-Cilantro Cheez Sauce

2 cups tomato salsa

½ cup nutritional yeast flakes

¼ cup sesame tahini

2 to 4 tablespoons cashew butter

1½ teaspoons onion powder

½ teaspoon salt, or to taste

½ teaspoon ground coriander

¼ teaspoon garlic powder

½ cup chopped fresh cilantro, or to taste

Place all ingredients, except cilantro, in a food processor and process several minutes until smooth and creamy. Stir or pulse in fresh cilantro.

MAKES ABOUT 1½ CUPS

Try this delectable, creamy sauce on potatoes, noodles, vegetables, or grains. It's the perfect sour cream replacement for dairy and soy-sensitive individuals. Use cold water for a cold sauce, or hot water for an instant, no-cook warm sauce.

FREE OF: GLUTEN SOY YEAST CORN	Per ¼ cup:	
	calories	126
	protein	4 g
	fat	11 g
	carbohydrate	6 g
	calcium	10 mg
	sodium	3 mg

MAKES ABOUT 2½ CUPS

Using salsa prepared with roasted tomatoes or chipotle peppers will impart a tempting smoky essence.

FREE OF: GLUTEN SOY CORN	Per ¼ cup:	
	calories	89
	protein	5 g
	fat	6 g
	carbohydrate	7 g
	calcium	96 mg
	sodium	290 mg

MAKES ABOUT ¼ CUP

When you've got to have your cheez right now, this is the sauce for you. It makes enough for one generous serving, but the recipe can be easily doubled, tripled, or quadrupled. It isn't necessary to heat this sauce. Just mix it in a bowl and drizzle it over cooked elbow macaroni, baked potatoes, rice, or steamed broccoli. The heat of the other food will warm it sufficiently—no waiting required! The basic sauce appeals more to younger palates; adults will enjoy any or all of the optional additions.

Minute-Man Cheez Sauce

Basic Minute–Man Cheez Sauce

2 tablespoons nutritional yeast flakes

1 tablespoon sesame tahini

1 teaspoon ketchup, tomato sauce, or pizza sauce

Salt

¼ cup water

Optional Additions

1 teaspoon extra-virgin olive oil

1 teaspoon light or chick-pea miso

1 teaspoon balsamic vinegar

1 teaspoon additional ketchup, tomato sauce, or pizza sauce

¼ teaspoon crushed garlic or garlic powder to taste

Pinch of dry mustard, or ¼ teaspoon prepared mustard

Crushed hot red pepper flakes, Tabasco, or cayenne

In a small bowl, combine yeast, tahini, ketchup, and salt to taste. Gradually stir in the water, using a fork or mini–whisk, beating until smooth. Beat in optional additions as desired.

Variations

• Ketchup may be omitted, if desired.

• Tamari or umeboshi vinegar may be used instead of or in addition to the salt.

Per ¼ cup:	
calories	138
protein	11 g
fat	8 g
carbohydrate	11 g
calcium	74 mg
sodium	75 mg

FREE
OF:
GLUTEN
SOY
NUTS
CORN

Contains sesame tahini.

Instant Cheez-It
(dry sauce mix)

2 cups mix		4 cups mix
1 cup	flour (any kind)	2 cups
1 cup	nutritional yeast flakes	2 cups
2 teaspoons	salt	4 teaspoons
1 teaspoon	onion powder	2 teaspoons
1 teaspoon	paprika	2 teaspoons
½ teaspoon	garlic powder	1 teaspoon
½ teaspoon	dry mustard	1 teaspoon

Combine ingredients in a jar or plastic container with a tight-fitting lid or in a zippered bag. Seal container and shake until evenly combined. Shake again before each use to combine ingredients that may have settled. Store mix in an airtight container or zippered bag at room temperature. Will keep indefinitely.

To make 1 cup Cheez–It Sauce:

Place ½ cup dry sauce mix in a small saucepan. With a fork or wire whisk, gradually beat in 1 cup water or plain nondairy milk. Work slowly to avoid lumps. Cook and stir over medium heat until smooth, thick, and bubbly. If desired, stir in 1 teaspoon vegetable oil (olive, sesame, or other) or non–hydrogenated vegan margarine. Mix well. Serve hot.

Tip: For enhanced sharpness, add a pinch of citric acid powder, to taste.

MAKES 2 OR 4 CUPS DRY MIX (enough for about 5 or 10 cups sauce)

Making quick cheez sauce has never been easier than with this handy pre-mixed powder. Just add water and oil or margarine, if desired, heat, and serve. This may just become the most important staple in your uncheese repertoire!

FREE OF:
GLUTEN
SOY
NUTS
CORN

Per ½ cup (sauce):	
calories	78
protein	8 g
fat	1 g
carbohydrate	13 g
calcium	8 mg
sodium	430 mg

Melty White Cheez

Pour this thick, luscious sauce over steamed vegetables, baked potatoes, macaroni (for instant macaroni and cheez), toast points, or corn chips, or drizzle it over pizza or casseroles before or after baking. You can even give this a curry flavor by blending in ½ teaspoon of curry powder.

1½ cups water or plain nondairy milk

¼ cup nutritional yeast flakes

¼ cup flour (any kind; your choice)

2 tablespoons sesame tahini

2 tablespoons kuzu, arrowroot, or cornstarch

2 teaspoons fresh lemon juice

1 teaspoon onion powder

¾ teaspoon salt

¼ teaspoon garlic powder

Place all ingredients in a blender and process until completely smooth. Transfer to a small saucepan. Cook over medium-high heat, stirring almost constantly with a wire whisk until very thick and smooth. Serve hot.

Smoky Melty Cheez: Reduce salt to ½ teaspoon, and blend in 1 tablespoon light or chickpea miso and a few drops liquid hickory smoke to taste.

Chili Melty Cheez: Stir in ¼ cup canned green chilies, or minced fresh chilies (hot or mild) to taste.

Orange Melty Cheez: Blend in ¼ to ½ teaspoon hot or sweet paprika.

Swiss Melty Cheez: Blend in 2 teaspoons light or chickpea miso.

Melty Chedda Cheez: Reduce salt to ½ teaspoon, and blend in 2 teaspoons light or chickpea miso, ¼ to ½ teaspoon paprika, and ¼ teaspoon dry mustard.

Spicy Melty Cheez: Blend in ¼ teaspoon cayenne, several drops Tabasco, or 1 small hot chili, seeded and chopped.

Per ¼ cup:	
calories	85
protein	5 g
fat	3 g
carbohydrate	11 g
calcium	31 mg
sodium	326 mg

FREE OF:
GLUTEN
SOY
NUTS
CORN

Contains sesame tahini.

All-American Cheez Sauce

MAKES ABOUT 2½ CUPS

This lightly seasoned, mild and cheezy sauce is popular with children and adults who prefer more mellow tastes. It's great on noodles, vegetables, or potatoes, and makes a delicious topping for casseroles, burgers, and loaves. Oil or margarine may be added for a richer sauce or omitted if you prefer your sauce fat free.

2¼ cups water or plain nondairy milk

½ cup cooked chopped carrots or winter squash

½ cup nutritional yeast flakes

½ cup flour (any kind; your choice)

2 tablespoons olive oil or nonhydrogenated vegan margarine (optional)

1 tablespoon fresh lemon juice

2 teaspoons onion powder

2 teaspoons salt

Place all ingredients in a blender and process until completely smooth and no orange flecks remain. Transfer to a medium saucepan. Bring to a boil stirring constantly with a wire whisk. Reduce heat and cook over medium, stirring almost constantly with a wire whisk until very thick and smooth. Serve hot.

No–Bake Macaroni and Cheez

Pour hot sauce over cooked elbow macaroni. Top with toasted breadcrumbs, or breadcrumbs or sliced almonds sautéed in olive oil or margarine, if desired.

Speedy Cheez and Vegetable Soup

Thin sauce with a small amount of plain nondairy milk, vegetable broth, or water and add your favorite cooked vegetables (fresh or frozen).

FREE OF:
GLUTEN
SOY
NUTS
CORN

Per ½ cup:	
calories	85
protein	8 g
fat	1 g
carbohydrate	14 g
calcium	12 mg
sodium	861 mg

Enjoy this all-purpose cheez sauce on noodles, vegetables, grains, or potatoes. It also makes a delicious sauce for casseroles, burgers, and loaves.

Warm Cheez Wiz Sauce

½ cup flour (any kind; your choice)

½ cup nutritional yeast flakes

½ teaspoon onion powder

½ teaspoon hot or sweet paprika

¼ teaspoon garlic powder

¼ teaspoon dry mustard

2 cups water or plain nondairy milk

¼ cup olive oil

1 teaspoon light or chickpea miso

Salt

Combine flour, yeast flakes, onion powder, paprika, garlic powder, and dry mustard in a medium saucepan. Gradually whisk in the water or milk, olive oil, and miso. Cook over medium heat, stirring almost constantly with a wire whisk until bubbly, thick, and smooth. Season with salt to taste.

Per ½ cup:

calories	219
protein	10 g
fat	14 g
carbohydrate	16 g
calcium	10 mg
sodium	39 mg

FREE OF:
GLUTEN
SOY
NUTS
CORN

Quick and Easy Alfredo Sauce

2 cups plain nondairy milk

1½ cups (about 12 ounces) crumbled firm silken tofu

1 teaspoon onion powder

½ teaspoon garlic powder

½ teaspoon salt

Pinch of grated nutmeg

1 cup Parmezano Sprinkles, page 50, or soy-based vegan
   parmesan alternative

Combine all ingredients, except Parmezano Sprinkles, in a blender or food processor, and process until very smooth and creamy. Transfer mixture to a medium saucepan, and cook and stir over low heat until warmed through. Do not boil. Remove from heat and stir in Parmezano Sprinkles. Adjust seasonings, if necessary. Serve at once.

MAKES ABOUT 4 CUPS

Use this amazing yet simple sauce to top pasta, vegetables, potatoes, or grains.

FREE OF:
GLUTEN
NUTS
YEAST
CORN

Per ½ cup:	
calories	152
protein	12 g
fat	10 g
carbohydrate	6 g
calcium	124 mg
sodium	241 mg

This recipe is very adaptable, so feel free to experiment with whatever herbs, spices, and seasonings you have on hand. This is the ultimate sauce for macaroni and cheez, but it's also terrific poured over toast points to make rarebit (try adding a dash of vegan Worcestershire sauce or balsamic vinegar) or generously spooned over potatoes.

Amazing Mac 'N Cheez Sauce

½ cup flour (any kind; your choice)

½ cup nutritional yeast flakes

1 teaspoon salt

¼ teaspoon onion powder

¼ teaspoon garlic powder

¼ teaspoon hot or sweet paprika

2 cups water or plain nondairy milk

¼ cup olive oil

½ teaspoon prepared mustard (any kind; your choice)

Combine flour, yeast flakes, salt, onion powder, garlic powder, and paprika in a medium saucepan. Gradually whisk in the water or milk, olive oil, and mustard. Cook over medium heat, stirring almost constantly with a wire whisk until bubbly, thick, and smooth.

Per ½ cup:	
calories	173
protein	8 g
fat	11 g
carbohydrate	14 g
calcium	8 mg
sodium	436 mg

FREE OF:
GLUTEN
SOY
NUTS
CORN

Nacho Cheez Sauce and Dip

½ cup flour (any kind; your choice)

½ cup nutritional yeast flakes

1 teaspoon salt

1 teaspoon chili powder

½ teaspoon onion powder

½ teaspoon hot or sweet paprika

¼ teaspoon garlic powder

¼ teaspoon dried oregano

⅛ to ¼ teaspoon cayenne

2 cups water or plain nondairy milk

¼ cup olive oil

½ teaspoon prepared mustard (any kind; your choice)

½ teaspoon light or chickpea miso

¼ cup minced fresh cilantro (optional)

Serve this zippy cheez sauce with corn tortillas or taco chips. It's also fantastic over steamed baby potatoes and vegetables.

Combine the flour, yeast flakes, salt, chili powder, onion powder, paprika, garlic powder, oregano, and cayenne in a medium saucepan. Gradually whisk in the water or milk, olive oil, and mustard. Cook over medium heat, stirring almost constantly with a wire whisk, until bubbly, thick, and smooth. Remove from the heat and whisk in the miso. Stir in the cilantro, if using, just before serving.

FREE OF:
GLUTEN
SOY
NUTS
CORN

Per ½ cup:

calories	97
protein	4 g
fat	6 g
carbohydrate	7 g
calcium	4 mg
sodium	250 mg

65

MAKES ABOUT 2½ CUPS

White beans make this sauce extra creamy and rich-tasting while keeping fat to a minimum.

Luscious Low-Fat Cheez Sauce

2 cups water or plain nondairy milk

½ cup drained cooked or canned white beans

½ cup flour (any kind; your choice)

½ cup nutritional yeast flakes

1 tablespoon olive oil or organic canola or safflower oil

1 teaspoon salt

½ teaspoon prepared mustard (any kind; your choice)

¼ teaspoon onion powder

¼ teaspoon garlic powder

¼ teaspoon hot or sweet paprika

Combine all ingredients in blender and process several minutes until completely smooth. Transfer to a medium saucepan and cook over medium heat, stirring almost constantly with a wire whisk until bubbly, thick, and smooth.

Per ½ cup:	
calories	127
protein	10 g
fat	3 g
carbohydrate	17 g
calcium	24 mg
sodium	437 mg

FREE OF:
GLUTEN
SOY
NUTS
CORN

"Say Cheez" Gravy

MAKES 2½ CUPS

½ cup flour (any kind; your choice)

½ cup nutritional yeast flakes

¾ teaspoon salt

Pepper

1½ cups plain nondairy milk

1 cup vegetable broth or water

2 tablespoons balsamic vinegar

2 tablespoons sherry (optional)

A quick, delicious gravy for baked or mashed potatoes, biscuits, tempeh, seitan, burgers, or loaves. It stores well in the refrigerator for several days, but it will thicken as it cools. If it becomes too thick for your liking, simply whisk in an additional tablespoon or two of nondairy milk, vegetable broth, water, or sherry when you reheat it.

Place flour, nutritional yeast, salt, and pepper in medium saucepan and stir to combine. Gradually whisk in milk, beating well to avoid lumps. Whisk in remaining ingredients until very smooth. Bring to a boil over medium–high heat, stirring constantly. Reduce heat to low and cook, stirring almost constantly with the wire whisk until thick, hot, and bubbly, about 5 minutes.

FREE OF:
GLUTEN
SOY
NUTS
CORN

Per ½ cup:	
calories	102
protein	10 g
fat	2 g
carbohydrate	14 g
calcium	11 mg
sodium	332 mg

MAKES ABOUT 1⅓ CUPS

Astound yourself and your family and friends with this mouth-watering, no-cook, dairy-free sauce. It can be on the table before you know it and will add a touch of scrumptious cheezy flavor to all your special creations. Beyond the traditional applications for cheese sauce, try this one as a salad dressing, a dip for oven fries or carrot sticks, or the finishing touch for casseroles just before serving.

I Can't Believe It's Not Cheese Sauce

⅓ cup sesame tahini

2 tablespoons nutritional yeast flakes

2 tablespoons fresh lemon juice

2 tablespoons light or chickpea miso

1½ to 2 teaspoons onion powder

¼ to ½ teaspoon salt

⅔ cup water

In a small bowl, cream together tahini, nutritional yeast, lemon juice, miso, onion powder, and salt. Gradually stir in the water using a fork or whisk, beating well until smooth.

Variations

• For a smoky flavor, add a few drops liquid hickory smoke.

• For a light orange–colored sauce, add ¼ teaspoon paprika (sweet or hot).

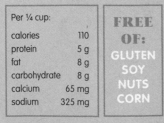

Per ¼ cup:	
calories	110
protein	5 g
fat	8 g
carbohydrate	8 g
calcium	65 mg
sodium	325 mg

FREE OF:
GLUTEN
SOY
NUTS
CORN

Contains sesame tahini.

Hot or Cold Tangy Chedda Sauce

MAKES 2 CUPS

Pour this delectable golden sauce over split baked potatoes topped with broccoli or your favorite steamed veggies, or drizzle it over baked tortilla chips as a quick nacho topping. It's delicious served either hot or cold.

¼ cup raw cashews

1 cup water or plain nondairy milk

1 cup roasted red peppers (skin and seeds removed), or pimiento pieces

⅓ cup nutritional yeast flakes

¼ cup sesame tahini

3 tablespoons fresh lemon juice

2 teaspoons onion powder

¾ teaspoon salt

¼ teaspoon garlic powder

¼ teaspoon ground coriander

⅛ teaspoon ground allspice

Grind cashews finely in an electric coffee grinder or herb mill or in a dry blender. Place ground cashews and remaining ingredients in a blender and process several minutes until smooth and creamy. To serve hot, warm over medium heat, stirring almost constantly until hot, thickened, and bubbly. To serve cold, chill after blending.

FREE OF:
GLUTEN
SOY
CORN

Per ¼ cup:	
calories	89
protein	5 g
fat	6 g
carbohydrate	6 g
calcium	38 mg
sodium	208 mg

This sauce is incredible over pasta, rice, or potatoes, and is particularly striking served with blue corn chips. For authentic flavor, stir in some freshly chopped cilantro just before serving or sprinkle it on as a garnish.

Per ½ cup:		FREE OF:
calories	91	GLUTEN
protein	6 g	SOY
fat	2 g	NUTS
carbohydrate	14 g	CORN
calcium	145 mg	
sodium	390 mg	

Contains sesame tahini.

This is the quintessential cheez sauce for broccoli, cauliflower, or potatoes. It's also perfect for nachos!

Per ¼ cup:		FREE OF:
calories	84	GLUTEN
protein	6 g	SOY
fat	2 g	NUTS
carbohydrate	11 g	CORN
calcium	39 mg	
sodium	99 mg	

Contains sesame tahini.

Nippy Tomato Non-Queso Sauce

2 cups tomato salsa

1 cup Gee Whiz Spread, p. 39

Stir together salsa and spread until well combined. Serve at room temperature or place in a medium saucepan and heat gently over low, stirring almost constantly until warm.

Quick and Creamy Non-Queso Sauce

2 cups Gee Whiz Spread, p. 39

1 cup plain nondairy milk

Combine spread and milk in a medium saucepan and heat gently over low, stirring almost constantly until warm.

Chili Non–Queso Sauce

Stir in 12 ounces canned, chopped green chilies and an additional ½ teaspoon onion powder.

Fiery Non–Queso Sauce

Stir in a good sized pinch of cayenne, several drops of Tabasco, or 1 small hot chili, seeded and finely chopped.

CHEEZY SOUPS, STEWS, AND CHOWDERS

The majority of the soups in this section will keep in the refrigerator for seven to ten days, and if you make a big batch you can use it handily for meals throughout the week. You'll also be pleased to know that most of these gorgeous soups are surprisingly quick and simple to prepare. Reheating soup (or any food, for that matter) more than once makes it prone to foodborne pathogens. When warming leftover soup, always reheat it close to the boiling point for the sake of food safety as well as the best flavor. Cheezy soups that contain pasta or potatoes or are starch-thickened do not freeze well, as they tend to lose their texture (even though the soup's flavor will remain intact). Thick, leftover cheez soups can become very stew-like, making them ideal for topping grains, pasta, or potatoes to create a quick and satisfying meal. A great soup is soothing and satisfying, whether as a midday lunch or a light evening meal. Just add some whole-grain bread, crackers, or crusty rolls and a salad and your feast is complete. Some cultures even enjoy soup for breakfast. Leftover soup can be heated and put in a thermos for meals away from home or warmed in the microwave oven for lunch at the office. With this convenience, you'll only have to put in the real effort once.

If your household is small, you can still make a large quantity and then freeze it in individual serving-size containers. Frozen soup can be defrosted in the refrigerator or microwave. When reheating leftover soup, just take out the quantity you'll be using at that particular meal.

Special Note:

• If you are unable to have gluten, always use a gluten-free flour (such as chickpea or rice flour) with any recipe in this section that calls for flour. Gluten-free options will not affect the outcome of the soups, stews, or chowders.

This thick, rich, creamy soup is very easy to make and highly nutritious. Use any combination of carrots, kale, zucchini, and cabbage that you like. It makes a large quantity, but leftovers store well in the refrigerator. Just reheat them carefully so the soup doesn't curdle or burn.

See photo, facing p. 97

Per cup:		FREE OF:
calories	92	GLUTEN
protein	3 g	SOY
fat	5 g	NUTS
carbohydrate	10 g	YEAST
calcium	66 mg	CORN
sodium	327 mg	

Contains sesame tahini.

Creamy Vegetable Chowder

10 cups vegetable broth or water

⅔ cup short-grain brown rice

2 teaspoons crushed garlic

2 teaspoons grated fresh gingerroot

6 cups mixed vegetables: diced carrots, thinly sliced kale, diced zucchini, thinly sliced green or Chinese cabbage (keep each vegetable separate)

½ cup sesame tahini

3 tablespoons light or chickpea miso

3 tablespoons tamari or balsamic vinegar

1 cup water

Salt and pepper

Combine the 10 cups broth or water, rice, garlic, and ginger–root in a large soup pot and bring to a boil. Reduce heat to medium–low, cover, and cook 45 minutes. Add carrots and kale and cover and cook 8 to 10 minutes. Add zucchini and cabbage and cover and cook 5 minutes more or until all vegetables are tender. Combine tahini, miso, and tamari or vinegar in a bowl. Slowly stir in 1 cup water, mixing into a smooth paste. Gradually stir paste into soup, mixing until creamy. Season with salt and pepper to taste. Thin with a little extra water if too thick. Do not boil.

Philly Potato Chowder

Dig into this hearty soup any time of the year. It's loaded with potatoes and has a delightful cream cheese-flavored base.

8 cups vegetable broth or water

5 cups peeled and diced potatoes

2 large onions, diced

1½ cups sliced scallions

1 cup plain nondairy milk

¾ cup raw cashews

⅓ cup flour (any kind; your choice)

¼ cup nutritional yeast flakes

2½ teaspoons salt

2 teaspoons onion powder

2 teaspoons garlic powder

1 tablespoon vegetarian bacon bits

Combine broth or water, potatoes, and onions in a large soup pot and bring to a boil. Lower heat, cover, and simmer until potatoes are fork tender and begin to break down, about 30 minutes. Remove from heat and stir in scallions.

Remove 2 cups of the soup broth with some of the vegetables in it, and place in a blender with remaining ingredients, except the vegetarian bacon bits. Process until completely smooth. Return blended mixture to soup pot. Cook and stir over medium heat until thickened. Stir in vegetarian bacon bits. Serve hot, but do not boil.

FREE OF:
GLUTEN
SOY
CORN

Per cup:	
calories	115
protein	4 g
fat	4 g
carbohydrate	17 g
calcium	20 mg
sodium	349 mg

Note: Most vegetarian bacon bits contain soy, and many also contain gluten. Read package labels carefully. Omit if necessary, or replace with hickory salt or a few drops of liquid hickory smoke, if desired. Add to mixture during blending. If using hickory salt, reduce or omit other salt.

MAKES 5 CUPS

Creamy cheddar cheese soup was a childhood favorite, so I was compelled to create a dairy-free version that was as velvety and rich-tasting as the one I fondly remember. Although the standard recipe is delicious in its own right, the variations that follow add even more excitement, and they're a tasty way to entice young ones to eat their vegetables.

Per cup:	
calories	181
protein	19 g
fat	4 g
carbohydrate	22 g
calcium	53 mg
sodium	582 mg

FREE OF:
GLUTEN
SOY
NUTS
CORN

Cheez Please Soup

1 large potato, peeled and diced

1 large carrot, coarsely chopped

1 large onion, coarsely chopped

1 cup vegetable broth or water

1½ cups (12 ounces) crumbled firm silken tofu or drained cooked or canned white beans (one 15-ounce can)

½ to 1 cup nutritional yeast flakes

2 tablespoons fresh lemon juice

2 tablespoons olive oil or nonhydrogenated vegan margarine (optional)

1¼ teaspoons salt

1 teaspoon onion powder

¼ teaspoon garlic powder

1 cup plain nondairy milk, vegetable broth, or water

Combine the potato, carrot, onion, and vegetable broth in a large soup pot and bring to a boil. Reduce the heat, cover, and simmer, stirring once or twice, until the vegetables are tender.

Combine the tofu, nutritional yeast flakes, lemon juice, olive oil, salt, onion powder, and garlic powder in a large bowl. Mix well and stir into the cooked vegetables. Purée the mixture in batches in a blender. Process until completely smooth. Pour the blended mixture into a clean soup pot and add each blended batch to it as it is finished. Stir in the milk, and warm the soup over low heat until hot (do not boil). If too thick, add additional milk, broth, or water to achieve the desired consistency. Adjust seasonings, if necessary.

Broccoli or Cauliflower Cheez Soup

Add 1½ to 2 cups steamed, bite-size broccoli or cauliflower florets.

Cheezy Vegetable Soup

Add one 10-ounce package mixed frozen vegetables, cooked according to package directions and drained well.

Green Peas and Cheez Soup

Add ½ cups frozen, loose-pack green peas, cooked according to package directions and drained well.

Herbed Cheez Please Soup

Add 1 to 1½ teaspoons of your favorite dried herb or 2 tablespoons chopped fresh herb. Herbs may also be added to the other variations above. Dillweed is particularly compatible with green peas. Thyme or oregano is a good match with mixed vegetables. Basil is a tasty complement to broccoli.

The flavor and aroma of the exotic spices in this thick and hearty soup are absolutely tantalizing— they lift the spirit and soothe the soul.

Per cup:	
calories	111
protein	7 g
fat	5 g
carbohydrate	12 g
calcium	54 mg
sodium	328 mg

FREE OF:
GLUTEN
SOY
NUTS
CORN

Contains sesame tahini.

Curried Cauliflower Cheez Soup

6 cups vegetable broth or water

1 large head cauliflower, broken into bite-size florets

1 large onion, diced

1 cup diced celery

2 cups plain nondairy milk or water

½ cup sesame tahini

½ cup nutritional yeast flakes

½ cup flour (any kind; your choice)

3 tablespoons fresh lemon juice or balsamic vinegar

2 tablespoons grated fresh gingerroot

1 tablespoon ground cumin

1 tablespoon ground coriander

2 teaspoons turmeric

2 teaspoons salt

1 teaspoon ground cinnamon

1 teaspoon crushed garlic

¼ teaspoon each: pepper, cayenne, ground cloves

1 cup frozen green peas, thawed

1 tablespoon dried dillweed

Combine broth or water, cauliflower, onion, and celery in a large soup pot and bring to a boil. Reduce heat, cover, and simmer, stirring occasionally, until cauliflower is tender, about 10 to 15 minutes. Combine remaining ingredients, except peas and dillweed, in a blender and process until very smooth. Pour into soup pot with cooked vegetables. Stir in peas and dillweed. Cook and stir until thickened and flour no longer tastes raw. Do not boil. Adjust seasonings if needed. Serve hot.

Zucchini Chedda Soup

MAKES 3½ QUARTS

8 cups vegetable broth or water

6 medium zucchini, diced

1 large onion, diced

1 cup roasted red peppers (skin and seeds removed)
  or pimiento pieces

½ to 1 cup nutritional yeast flakes

½ cup sesame tahini

½ cup flour (any kind; your choice)

½ cup raw cashews

¼ cup tamari, or 2 tablespoons balsamic vinegar*

3 tablespoons fresh lemon juice

1 tablespoon dried oregano

Salt, to taste

½ to 1 teaspoon crushed garlic

½ teaspoon ground allspice

½ teaspoon pepper

Cheese lovers will adore this tempting soup. It's jam-packed with delicate zucchini and loads of hearty flavor. You can easily make Zucchini, Chedda, and Rice Soup by adding 1 cup cooked rice to the soup while it is heating.

Combine broth or water, zucchini, and onion in a large soup pot and bring to a boil. Reduce heat, cover, and simmer, stirring once or twice until vegetables are very tender, about 20 minutes.

Place 2 cups of the soup broth, including some of the cooked onion and zucchini, in a blender with the remaining ingredients. Process until very smooth. Stir blended mixture back into soup pot with remaining broth and vegetables. Heat gently, stirring often, until slightly thickened and warmed through, about 10 minutes. Do not boil. Serve hot.

*Note: If using balsamic vinegar, reduce the lemon juice to 1 or 2 tablespoons, or to taste.

FREE OF:
GLUTEN
SOY
CORN

Per cup:	
calories	130
protein	7 g
fat	7 g
carbohydrate	13 g
calcium	54 mg
sodium	316 mg

MAKES 6 SERVINGS

This French classic is known for its gooey topping of luscious cheeses. This one rivals the best!

French Onion Soup Gruyère

1 tablespoon olive oil

2 large or 3 medium onions, thinly sliced or chopped

1½ teaspoons crushed garlic

¼ cup flour (any kind; your choice)

4 cups vegetable broth or water

¼ cup low-sodium tamari

Gruyère Cheez Topping

1 cup water

2 tablespoons fresh lemon juice

2 tablespoons sesame tahini

2 tablespoons nutritional yeast flakes

2 tablespoons flour (any kind; your choice)

4 teaspoons kuzu, arrowroot, or cornstarch

1½ teaspoons onion powder

¼ teaspoon salt

Additional Ingredients

French bread (1 slice per serving), or ¼ cup croutons per serving

¼ cup Parmezano Sprinkles, page 50, or soy-based vegan parmesan alternative

Heat oil in a large soup pot over medium–high. When hot, add onions and garlic and sauté 5 minutes. Stir in flour, mixing well. Stir in broth or water and tamari and bring to a boil. Reduce heat to low, cover, and simmer until onions are very tender, about 20 minutes.

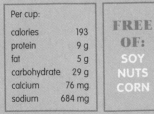

Per cup:	
calories	193
protein	9 g
fat	5 g
carbohydrate	29 g
calcium	76 mg
sodium	684 mg

FREE OF:
SOY
NUTS
CORN

Contains sesame tahini.

To make a Gruyère cheez topping, place the 1 cup water, lemon juice, tahini, nutritional yeast, flour, kuzu or arrowroot, onion powder, and salt in a blender. Process several minutes until completely smooth. Pour into a small saucepan and cook and stir over medium heat until smooth and thick, about 5 to 8 minutes. Cover and set aside.

Place a slice of French bread or some croutons in the bottom of each soup bowl. Ladle soup over the bread. Top each serving with several spoonfuls of the Gruyère cheeze, and sprinkle with 2 teaspoons of the Parmezano Sprinkles. Serve at once. Pass more Parmezano Sprinkles at the table, if desired.

Variation

For browned Gruyère cheez, place bread on a dry baking sheet. Spread with cheez and place briefly under boiler until golden brown. Transfer to soup bowls with a spatula and top with Parmezano Sprinkles. Alternatively, ladle soup into broiler-proof bowls and top with bread and Gruyère cheez. Place briefly under broiler until cheez is bubbly and golden brown. Sprinkle with Parmezano Sprinkles after removing from the oven.

MAKES ABOUT 4 QUARTS

What a tasty and quick way to serve eggplant! Tender vegetables and nutritious white beans mingle in a rich, creamy broth. If you prefer an even thicker stew, add a cup or two of cooked pasta or rice shortly before serving.

Per cup:		
calories	101	
protein	8 g	
fat	1 g	
carbohydrate	18 g	
calcium	64 mg	
sodium	38 mg	

FREE OF:
GLUTEN
SOY
NUTS
CORN

Eggplant Parmagiano Stew

8 cups vegetable broth or water

1 (6-ounce) can tomato paste

1 tablespoon crushed garlic

1 medium eggplant, unpeeled and diced

2 cups finely chopped, packed kale

1 large onion, chopped

4 cups drained cooked or canned white beans
   (two 15- or 16-ounce cans)

½ cup nutritional yeast flakes

2 teaspoons dried oregano

2 fresh tomatoes, chopped

Salt, pepper, and cayenne

Parmezano Sprinkles, p. 50, or soy-based vegan
   parmesan alternative (optional)

Combine broth or water, tomato paste, and garlic in a large soup pot. Add eggplant, onion, and kale. Bring to a boil. Reduce heat, cover, and simmer gently until eggplant is tender but firm, about 15 minutes. Place 2 cups soup broth, 2 cups beans, nutritional yeast, and oregano in blender and process until very smooth. Pour into soup pot with vegetables and mix well. Stir in remaining 2 cups of beans and fresh tomatoes. Season with salt, pepper, and cayenne to taste. Simmer uncovered until beans are heated through and tomatoes are slightly softened. Garnish each serving with Parmezano Sprinkles or soy-based vegan parmesan alternative, if desired.

FONDUES

In addition to being a welcome meal when time and energy are in short supply, uncheese fondues make terrific fare for intimate parties or romantic dinners. They are both fun and sophisticated. Preparation is easy; service and cleanup are a breeze.

The most straightforward way to serve fondue is to give each diner a small plate and a fondue fork. Then, fill small bowls or baskets with bite-size items to dunk into the fondue. Arrange the bowls around the table for easy reaching or passing. Bread cubes; bagel pieces; raw, steamed, or grilled vegetables; steamed or boiled potatoes; veggie hot dogs, sausages, and other meat alternatives; chunks of seitan or cooked tempeh; firm smoked tofu; and even sections of fruit are well-suited options. Select dipping items that will complement the flavor of your fondue. With the right choices, fondue can be a complete and satisfying meal in itself.

• If you are unable to have gluten, always use a gluten-free flour (such as chickpea or rice flour) with any recipe in this section that calls for flour. Gluten-free options will not affect the outcome of the fondues.

MAKES 3½ CUPS
(about 6 servings)

Dive into this luxurious, cheddary fondue that blends the tang of cheez with the gusto of beer.

Pub Fondue

2 (12 ounce) bottles nonalcoholic lager beer (about 3 cups)

½ cup roasted red peppers (skin and seeds removed), or pimiento pieces

½ cup nutritional yeast flakes

½ cup raw cashews, or ⅓ cup cashew butter

⅓ cup quick-cooking rolled oats, or ¼ cup flour (any kind)

¼ cup kuzu, arrowroot, or cornstarch

1 tablespoon onion powder

1 teaspoon dry mustard

½ teaspoon crushed garlic

½ teaspoon salt

¼ teaspoon white pepper

Place all the ingredients in a blender and process several minutes until the mixture is completely smooth. Pour into a medium saucepan and bring to a boil, stirring constantly. Reduce heat to low, and continue to stir and cook a few minutes longer until thick and smooth. Transfer to a fondue pot and keep warm over a very low flame.

Danish Fondue

Omit the red peppers, salt, and white pepper. Use 1½ tablespoons onion powder and ½ teaspoon dry mustard. Follow directions for Pub Fondue above. Stir in 2 tablespoons vegetarian bacon bits just before transferring to fondue pot.

Swiss Fondue

3 cups water or plain nondairy milk

½ cup nutritional yeast flakes

⅓ cup quick-cooking rolled oats, or ¼ cup flour
(any kind; your choice)

¼ cup fresh lemon juice

¼ cup sesame tahini

¼ cup kuzu, arrowroot, or cornstarch

4 teaspoons onion powder

1 teaspoon salt

½ teaspoon dry mustard

Place all the ingredients in a blender and process several minutes until the mixture is completely smooth. Pour into a medium saucepan and bring to a boil, stirring constantly. Reduce heat to low, and continue to stir and cook a few minutes longer until thick and smooth. Transfer to a fondue pot and keep warm over a very low flame.

Vegan Swiss Raclette

Follow the recipe for Swiss Fondue, but spoon the thickened sauce onto individual serving plates so guests can spread it directly on bread or boiled potatoes, cooked pearl onions, and pickles. (Raclette is a popular Swiss snack or supper favorite made from melted cheese.)

**MAKES 3½ CUPS
(ABOUT 6 SERVINGS)**

This thick, cheezy sauce makes a superb dip for crusty, whole-grain bread cubes, seitan chunks, grilled tempeh, button mushrooms, broccoli and cauliflower florets, cherry tomatoes, and any other raw or lightly steamed vegetables.

**FREE OF:
GLUTEN
SOY
NUTS
CORN**

Per serving:	
calories	127
protein	8 g
fat	6 g
carbohydrate	15 g
calcium	54 mg
sodium	366 mg

Contains sesame tahini.

MAKES 3½ CUPS (ABOUT 6 SERVINGS)

This elegant cheez fondue has an appealing, sophisticated flavor.

Classic Fondue

2 cups nonalcoholic white wine

1 cup water or plain nondairy milk

½ cup nutritional yeast flakes

⅓ cup quick-cooking rolled oats, or ¼ cup flour (any kind)

¼ cup sesame tahini

¼ cup kuzu, arrowroot, or cornstarch

2 tablespoons fresh lemon juice

2 tablespoons onion powder

1 teaspoon salt

½ teaspoon dry mustard

Pinch each: white pepper and grated nutmeg

Place all the ingredients in a blender and process several minutes until the mixture is completely smooth. Pour into a medium saucepan and bring to a boil, stirring constantly. Reduce heat to low, and continue to stir and cook a few minutes longer until thick and smooth. Transfer to a fondue pot and keep warm over a very low flame.

Rosé Fondue

Replace the nonalcoholic white wine with an equal amount of nonalcoholic rosé or red wine.

Per serving:	
calories	180
protein	8 g
fat	6 g
carbohydrate	15 g
calcium	61 mg
sodium	370 mg

FREE OF:
GLUTEN
SOY
NUTS
CORN

Contains sesame tahini.

Chedda Fondue

MAKES 4 CUPS (ABOUT 7 TO 8 SERVINGS)

This opulent fondue is fabulous with button mushrooms, cauliflower chunks, bell pepper squares, and cubes of sesame or herb-seasoned whole-grain bread.

2¾ cups water or plain nondairy milk

1 cup roasted red peppers (skin and seeds removed), or pimiento pieces

½ cup nutritional yeast flakes

½ cup raw cashews, or ⅓ cup cashew butter

⅓ cup quick-cooking rolled oats, or ¼ cup flour (any kind; your choice)

¼ cup kuzu, arrowroot, or cornstarch

3 tablespoons fresh lemon juice

2 tablespoons sesame tahini

1 tablespoon onion powder

1 teaspoon salt

½ teaspoon dry mustard

½ teaspoon crushed garlic

¼ teaspoon Tabasco

¼ teaspoon each: paprika and grated nutmeg

Place all the ingredients in a blender and process several minutes until the mixture is completely smooth. Pour into a medium saucepan and bring to a boil, stirring constantly. Reduce heat to low, and continue to stir and cook a few minutes longer until thick and smooth. Transfer to a fondue pot and keep warm over a very low flame.

FREE OF:
GLUTEN
SOY
CORN

Per serving:	
calories	149
protein	8 g
fat	8 g
carbohydrate	16 g
calcium	34 mg
sodium	313 mg

MAKES 3½ CUPS
(ABOUT 6 SERVINGS)

This savory fondue is spiced with exotic chili seasonings. Try serving it with baby pickled corn, cucumber chunks, sweet red bell pepper squares, radishes, pitted black olives, stuffed green olives, and avocado pieces lightly sprinkled with fresh lime juice.

Per cup:	
calories	174
protein	8 g
fat	10 g
carbohydrate	16 g
calcium	58 mg
sodium	369 mg

FREE OF:
GLUTEN
SOY
NUTS
CORN

Contains sesame tahini.

86

South-of-the-Border Fondue

MAKES 3½ CUPS
(ABOUT 6 SERVINGS)

2 tablespoons olive oil

2 teaspoons crushed garlic

2 teaspoons paprika (hot or sweet)

1 teaspoon ground cumin

¼ teaspoon ground coriander

¼ teaspoon turmeric

Pinch of cayenne

3 cups water or plain nondairy milk

½ cup nutritional yeast flakes

⅓ cup quick-cooking rolled oats, or ¼ cup flour
    (any kind; your choice)

¼ cup kuzu, arrowroot, or cornstarch

¼ cup sesame tahini

¼ cup fresh lemon juice

2 tablespoons onion powder

1 teaspoon salt

½ teaspoon dry mustard

1 (4-ounce) can peeled and chopped green chilies

1 teaspoon dried oregano

½ teaspoon dried basil

¼ teaspoon dried marjoram

Heat oil in a large saucepan. When hot, add garlic and sauté until barely golden, about 30 seconds. Add paprika, cumin, coriander, turmeric, and cayenne and cook 20 seconds longer. Remove from heat.

Place water, nutritional yeast, oats or flour, kuzu or arrowroot, tahini, lemon juice, onion powder, salt, and mustard in a blender and process several minutes until oats are finely ground and sauce is completely smooth. Pour into saucepan with garlic and stir in chilies and remaining ingredients. Bring to a boil, stirring constantly. Reduce heat to low, and continue to stir and cook a few minutes longer until thick and smooth. Transfer to a fondue pot, and keep warm over a very low flame.

Smoky Fondue

2 (12 ounce) bottles nonalcoholic lager beer (about 3 cups)

½ cup chopped onions

½ cup nutritional yeast flakes

½ cup raw cashews, or ⅓ cup cashew butter

⅓ cup quick-cooking rolled oats, or ¼ cup flour (any kind; your choice)

¼ cup kuzu, arrowroot, or cornstarch

1 tablespoon spicy brown or Dijon mustard

½ teaspoon salt

½ teaspoon garlic powder

Several drops liquid hickory smoke

Place all the ingredients in a blender and process several minutes until the mixture is completely smooth. Pour into a medium saucepan and bring to a boil, stirring constantly. Reduce heat to low, and continue to stir and cook a few minutes longer until thick and smooth. Transfer to a fondue pot and keep warm over a very low flame.

MAKES 3½ CUPS (ABOUT 6 SERVINGS)

A gentle, smoky quality mingles with the full-bodied flavors of beer and onions in this captivating, luscious fondue. Serve it with whole-grain bread cubes and thick slices of cooked tofu frankfurters.

FREE OF: SOY CORN

Per serving:

calories	182
protein	9 g
fat	7 g
carbohydrate	19 g
calcium	23 mg
sodium	211 mg

87

Pizza Fondue

Lightly steamed baby mushrooms, pitted black olives, cherry tomatoes, sweet red bell pepper squares, cooked pearl onions, pepperoni-flavored veggie "meat," tofu sausages, and French bread cubes all make ideal accompaniments to this spicy "pizza in a pot."

1 tablespoon olive oil

1½ teaspoons crushed garlic

¼ teaspoon crushed red pepper flakes

3 cups water or plain nondairy milk

½ cup nutritional yeast flakes

⅓ cup quick-cooking rolled oats, or ¼ cup flour (any kind; your choice)

¼ cup sesame tahini

¼ cup kuzu, arrowroot, or cornstarch

¼ cup fresh lemon juice

¼ cup unsalted tomato paste

1 tablespoon onion powder

1½ teaspoons dried oregano

1 teaspoon salt

½ teaspoon dried basil

¼ to ½ teaspoon pepper

¼ teaspoon dried marjoram

Heat oil in a large saucepan. When hot, add garlic and sauté until barely golden, about 30 seconds. Add red pepper flakes, and cook 20 seconds longer. Remove from heat.

Place remaining ingredients in a blender and process several minutes until oats are finely ground and sauce is completely smooth. Pour into saucepan with garlic, mix well, and bring to a boil stirring constantly. Reduce heat to low, and continue to stir and cook a few minutes longer until thick and smooth. Transfer to a fondue pot and keep warm over a very low flame.

Sun-dried Tomato Fondue: Omit tomato paste and add ½ cup finely chopped sun-dried tomatoes or sun-dried tomato salad bits along with the red pepper flakes.

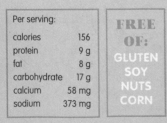

Per serving:		FREE OF:
calories	156	GLUTEN
protein	9 g	SOY
fat	8 g	NUTS
carbohydrate	17 g	CORN
calcium	58 mg	
sodium	373 mg	

Contains sesame tahini.

PASTA, POLENTA, AND OTHER MAIN DISHES

In this section, you'll find plenty of quick and cheesy main dishes to whet your appetite and please your palate. All the recipes are prepared on the stovetop. For oven-baked main dishes, refer to Quiches, Dinner Pies, Casseroles, and Soufflés, pages 101 through 122, and Pizzas, Breads, and Little Bites, pages 123 through 142.

The mild, unobtrusive taste of pasta and polenta melds beautifully with the sharp, full-bodied flavors of uncheese. If you are allergic to corn, substitute brown rice grits for polenta or cornmeal. If you cannot tolerate wheat or gluten, use rice (or corn or quinoa) pasta instead, and always use a gluten-free flour (such as chickpea or rice flour) whenever an option for flour is provided.

Most of these recipes need only a simple salad or steamed vegetable to complete the meal. That translates to less work and reduced preparation and cleanup time in the kitchen. What could be better?

Cheez-A-Roni

Almost everyone is fond of noodles, and elbow macaroni in a creamy, cheesy-tasting sauce always seems to top the list of favorites. This one has juicy tomato chunks in it and a delicious high-protein sauce. No one will guess it's made from beans, which makes it a terrific way to get wholesome food into picky eaters!

1 recipe (2 cups) Gee Whiz Spread, page 39, or Chick Cheeze, page 38

2 tablespoons olive oil

2 large onions, finely chopped

1 teaspoon crushed garlic

1 (28-ounce) can diced tomatoes, undrained

2 to 3 tablespoons nutritional yeast flakes

Salt to taste

¼ to ½ teaspoon pepper

Large pinch cayenne (optional)

3 cups (12 ounces) dry macaroni or other tube pasta (such as penne)

Prepare Gee Whiz Spread or Chick Cheez as directed and set aside. Heat oil in very large saucepan over medium–high heat. When hot, add onion and sauté until tender, deep brown, and caramelized (adjust heat as necessary so onion doesn't burn). Stir in garlic and cook for 1 minute longer. Add undrained tomatoes and stir. Then stir in the prepared Gee Whiz Spread or Chick Cheez, nutritional yeast flakes, salt, pepper, and cayenne (if using) and mix well. Simmer gently, stirring often, for about 10 to 15 minutes. Meanwhile, cook pasta according to package directions. Drain well. Stir hot pasta into simmering sauce and combine gently but thoroughly.

Tip: As this dish cools, or if there are leftovers stored in the refrigerator, the macaroni will absorb much of the moisture from the sauce. If you want to make the mixture more saucy, add a little tomato juice, plain nondairy milk, water, sherry, or 1 or 2 chopped, fresh tomatoes when you reheat it.

Per serving:	
calories	334
protein	16 g
fat	7 g
carbohydrate	55 g
calcium	99 mg
sodium	311 mg

FREE
OF:
GLUTEN
SOY
NUTS
CORN

Contains sesame tahini.

Noodles and Cottage Cheez

2 tablespoons olive oil

2 very large onions, chopped

1 pound bow tie or spiral noodles

1 pound firm regular tofu, mashed

1 cup vegan mayonnaise

Salt and pepper

Heat oil in a very large saucepan. When hot, add onions and sauté until tender , deep brown, and caramelized (adjust heat as necessary so onion doesn't burn). While onions are cooking, boil noodles according to package directions. Drain well. Stir into cooked onions and mix well. Stir in remaining ingredients, and season with salt and pepper to taste. Heat and stir over medium-low, watching closely so mixture doesn't stick to the bottom of the pan. Serve hot or warm.

MAKES 8 SERVINGS

This is a soothing and satisfying main dish. The special flavor comes from slow cooking the onions until they are very sweet and caramelized. It may take a little extra time, but the flavor and simplicity of the recipe make it well worth the wait.

FREE OF:
GLUTEN
NUTS
YEAST
CORN

Per serving:

calories	235
protein	8 g
fat	13 g
carbohydrate	20 g
calcium	68 mg
sodium	235 mg

MAKES 4 SERVINGS

This scrumptious pasta dish is considerably easier to make than regular stuffed shells. It's perfect for last-minute meals, and both children and adults love it. Serve it with a tossed green salad or calcium-rich greens, such as kale or broccoli.

Unstuffed Shells

1 pound firm regular tofu

⅓ to ½ cup vegan mayonnaise

2 to 3 tablespoons minced fresh parsley,
   or 1 tablespoon dried parsley flakes

2 teaspoons dried basil

2 teaspoons onion powder

1 teaspoon garlic powder

½ teaspoon salt

2 cups (one 16-ounce can) tomato sauce

4 cups medium shell pasta

Break tofu into large chunks. Place in a saucepan and cover with water. Bring to a boil, reduce heat, and simmer 5 minutes. Drain well and mash fine. Combine tofu, mayonnaise, and seasonings in a large bowl. Mix well and set aside. Heat tomato sauce in a small saucepan. Once hot, cover pot and keep warm on low heat. Cook pasta according to package directions. Drain well and combine with reserved tofu mixture, tossing gently until evenly distributed. Divide among four dinner plates. Top each serving with ¼ of the hot tomato sauce (about ½ cup per serving). Serve at once.

Per serving:

calories	369
protein	18 g
fat	12 g
carbohydrate	48 g
calcium	124 mg
sodium	736 mg

FREE OF:
GLUTEN
NUTS
YEAST
CORN

Fettuccine Alfonso

MAKES 6 SERVINGS

2 cups drained cooked or canned white beans
(one 15- or 16-ounce can)

1½ cups cooked and drained corn kernels
(fresh, frozen, or canned)

1½ cups plain nondairy milk or water

2 to 4 tablespoons sesame tahini (use the larger
amount if using water)

1 tablespoon onion powder

1 teaspoon salt

1 pound fettuccine noodles

Pepper and minced fresh parsley, basil,
or cilantro for garnish

This power-packed version of the classic Alfredo dish features the venerable ribbon noodle. Serve it with a crisp tossed salad and fresh Italian bread and your meal will be complete.

Divide beans in half. Place one half in blender and reserve the remainder. Add cooked corn, milk or water, tahini, onion pow-der, and salt to the blender and process several minutes until completely smooth. Pour into a medium saucepan and stir in reserved beans. Cook and stir over medium heat until sauce is hot and beans are heated through.

While sauce is heating, cook fettuccine according to package directions. Drain well and return to the pot. Add the hot sauce and toss until evenly coated. Serve immediately, garnished with pepper and fresh herbs.

Tip: For a completely smooth sauce, combine all of the beans in the blender. This also will make the sauce thicker.

FREE OF:
GLUTEN
SOY
NUTS
YEAST
CORN

Per serving:	
calories	305
protein	14 g
fat	6 g
carbohydrate	53 g
calcium	77 mg
sodium	451 mg

Contains sesame tahini.

MAKES 6 SERVINGS

Serve with a leafy green salad and perhaps some thinly sliced radishes and cucumbers.

Mediterranean Pasta

1 pound spaghetti

2 tablespoons olive oil

1 to 2 teaspoons crushed garlic

3 fresh tomatoes, coarsely chopped

½ cup sliced black olives

2 cups drained and crumbled Betta Feta, page 45

Pepper

Cook spaghetti according to package directions. Drain well and return to the pot or transfer to a large bowl. While pasta is cooking, heat oil in a medium skillet. When hot, add garlic and cook and stir 30 seconds only. Add chopped tomatoes and sauté just until slightly softened. Add to pasta along with olives, Betta Feta, and lots of pepper to taste. Toss gently but thoroughly. Serve at once.

Per serving:	
calories	261
protein	12 g
fat	11 g
carbohydrate	30 g
calcium	100 mg
sodium	725 mg

FREE OF:
GLUTEN
NUTS
YEAST
CORN

Noodles Ramona

MAKES 6 SERVINGS

This spin-off of the ever-popular Noodles Romanoff is an effortless, dairy-free rendering of the esteemed "pasta and cheddar" delight.

2 cups drained cooked or canned white beans
   (one 15- or 16-ounce can)

1 cup plain nondairy milk or water

½ cup roasted red peppers (skin and seeds removed)
   or pimiento pieces

½ cup nutritional yeast flakes

3 tablespoons fresh lemon juice

2 tablespoons sesame tahini (optional; include if using water)

½ teaspoon salt

1 pound thin fettuccine noodles

¼ cup minced fresh parsley

Combine beans, milk or water, peppers, nutritional yeast flakes, lemon juice, tahini (if using), and salt in a blender and purée several minutes until completely smooth. Pour into a medium saucepan and warm gently over low heat. Stir almost constantly, taking care not to boil.

Meanwhile, cook pasta according to package directions. Drain well and return to the pot or transfer to a large bowl. Pour warm sauce over pasta and toss well until evenly distributed. Garnish each serving with parsley.

FREE OF:
GLUTEN
SOY
NUTS
CORN

Per serving:

calories	244
protein	16 g
fat	2 g
carbohydrate	43 g
calcium	61 mg
sodium	191 mg

MAKES 4 TO 6 SERVINGS

Broccoli goes gourmet in this tantalizing pasta dish where it substitutes for fresh basil in an unusual but spectacular pesto.

Broccoli Pesto Pasta

6 to 7 cups broccoli florets (about 1 large bunch)

½ cup Parmezano Sprinkles, page 50,
   or soy-based vegan parmesan alternative

¼ cup water

2 tablespoons white wine vinegar or brown rice vinegar

2 tablespoons extra-virgin olive oil

2 teaspoons toasted sesame oil

½ teaspoon salt

½ teaspoon crushed garlic

12 ounces pasta (bow ties, spirals, or tubes)

1 small ripe tomato or 1 small raw or roasted red pepper,
   seeded and diced

To make the pesto, steam broccoli until tender. Place half the broccoli in a food processor along with the Parmezano Sprinkles, water, vinegar, oils, salt, and garlic. Process several minutes until creamy and smooth, stopping to scrape down sides of container as necessary. Add remaining broccoli and process again until smooth. Set aside.

Cook pasta according to package directions. Drain well. Combine with broccoli pesto and toss until evenly distributed. Garnish with tomato or roasted red pepper. Serve at once.

Tip: If not serving immediately, the pesto may be kept warm up to 30 minutes in a covered saucepan over very low heat.

Variation: For alternative garnish options, try grated carrot, paprika, or fresh basil.

Per serving:	
calories	229
protein	12 g
fat	9 g
carbohydrate	28 g
calcium	143 mg
sodium	450 mg

FREE
OF:
GLUTEN
SOY
NUTS
CORN

Contains vinegar.

Traditional Macaroni and Cheez, page 112

Bare Naked Polenta

1 cup yellow corn grits (polenta) or brown rice grits

½ teaspoon salt

3 cups water

Topping Options

• nonhydrogenated vegan margarine

• extra-virgin olive oil

• minced steamed vegetables

• chopped fresh herbs (basil, cilantro, dillweed, or parsley)

• grated block-style uncheese (pages 157 to 166)

Hot polenta is great for breakfast. It also makes an interesting main or side dish. Do not be tempted to substitute cornmeal for the corn grits because you will not have good results. Use only the more coarsely ground, whole grain grits, sometimes called polenta, which can be found in natural food stores and many supermarkets, or brown rice grits. This basic Italian staple traditionally is served with a marinara sauce, vegetables, or cheese.

In a medium saucepan, combine grits, salt, and 1 cup of the water to make a smooth paste. Gradually stir in remaining water. Bring to a boil stirring constantly. Lower heat and cook and stir until mixture is very thick and begins to pull away from the sides of the pan, about 20 to 30 minutes. Serve hot, bare naked (plain) or with one of the topping options above or variations below.

• **Italian or Cheddary Cheez Polenta:** Prepare Bare Naked Polenta as directed but omit salt. After polenta has finished cooking, beat in ½ cup Parmezano Sprinkles, page 50, or soy-based vegan parmesan alternative; ½ cup (or more, to taste) Gee Whiz Spread, page 39; or Chick Cheez, page 38. Heat through, if necessary. Serve at once.

• **Mammaliga:** (a satisfying, peasant-style polenta with cheez) Prepare Bare Naked Polenta as directed. Divide it among four serving bowls, and top each portion with 2 tablespoons Tofu Ricotta, page 46, or drained Betta Feta, page 45. Toss on a few sliced olives and sprinkle with fresh or dried dillweed.

Creamy Vegetable Chowder, page 72
Gooey Grilled Cheez Sandwich, page 141

FREE OF:	Per serving:	
GLUTEN	calories	62
SOY	protein	2 g
NUTS	fat	0 g
YEAST	carbohydrate	13 g
CORN	calcium	5 mg
	sodium	523 mg

MAKES **4** SERVINGS

Nutritional yeast flakes add cheese-like undertones to this delicious polenta, while broccoli adds flavor, nutrition, and beautiful flecks of green. To round out your dinner, serve the polenta with steamed carrots on the side or a platter of sliced tomatoes topped with fresh basil. Add a salad of baby greens dressed with a splash of balsamic vinegar and extra-virgin olive oil.

Cheezy Broccoli Polenta

5 cups water

1 to 2 cups finely chopped broccoli

1⅓ cups yellow corn grits (polenta) or brown rice grits

¼ cup nutritional yeast flakes

1 tablespoon olive oil

1 teaspoon salt

Bring water to a boil in a heavy-bottomed saucepan. Add broccoli and simmer until tender, about 5 minutes. Remove from the heat and slowly stir in the grits, stirring briskly with a long-handled wooden spoon. Return to a boil, stirring constantly. Reduce heat to very low, cover, and cook, stirring occasionally, until very thick, about 20 to 30 minutes. Vigorously stir in nutritional yeast flakes, olive oil, and salt and mix until well combined.

Tips: If the polenta sticks to the bottom of your saucepan, slip a heat diffuser underneath.

• For less stirring and sticking, after the grits and broccoli come to a boil, transfer the mixture to a double boiler to finish cooking.

Per serving:

calories	145
protein	7 g
fat	4 g
carbohydrate	22 g
calcium	28 mg
sodium	886 mg

FREE OF:
GLUTEN
SOY
NUTS
CORN

Eggplant Newburg

1 medium eggplant, peeled and cut into ½-inch dice

12 medium mushrooms, quartered

1 (32-ounce) can unsalted diced tomatoes, with juice

½ cup nonalcoholic sherry, nonalcoholic red or white wine,
  or mirin

¼ cup nutritional yeast flakes

¼ cup sesame tahini

2 tablespoons balsamic vinegar plus salt to taste,
  or 3 tablespoons tamari

Combine eggplant, mushrooms, tomatoes and their juice in a large skillet or wok and bring to a boil. Reduce heat to medium, cover, and simmer, stirring often, until eggplant is tender but still firm, about 25 to 30 minutes.

Stir together remaining ingredients until smooth. Turn off heat and stir tahini mixture into eggplant and tomatoes. Mix until well combined. Serve at once.

MAKES 6½ CUPS
(4 TO 6 SERVINGS)

This is an exciting yet easy way to serve eggplant. It is a perfect topping for grain and pasta, or serve it over split biscuits with a crisp salad on the side. Garnish it with cracked black pepper and fresh parsley, if desired.

FREE OF:
GLUTEN
SOY
NUTS
CORN

Per serving:	
calories	178
protein	9 g
fat	7 g
carbohydrate	19 g
calcium	109 mg
sodium	40 mg

Contains sesame tahini.

MAKES 32 BALLS
(ABOUT 8 SERVINGS)

These firm, tasty balls are amazingly versatile. They are delicious plain or served with ketchup, tomato sauce, or cocktail sauce. Try them on top of spaghetti and begin a new tradition. They are great cold as a snack or for lunch the following day on bread or a hot dog bun with a little ketchup or vegan mayonnaise.

Per serving:	
calories	216
protein	15 g
fat	11 g
carbohydrate	15 g
calcium	236 mg
sodium	506 mg

FREE OF:
GLUTEN
NUTS
YEAST
CORN

Spinafels
(Spinach Ricotta Balls)

1 pound firm regular tofu, well mashed

¾ cup vegan mayonnaise

½ cup yellow cornmeal or rice flour

⅓ cup flour (any kind; your choice)

2 teaspoons garlic powder

1 teaspoon onion powder

½ teaspoon salt

½ teaspoon dried oregano

½ teaspoon dried basil

Pepper

1 (10-ounce) package frozen chopped spinach,
    thawed and squeezed dry

⅔ cup Parmezano Sprinkles, page 50,
    or soy-based vegan parmesan alternative

Preheat oven to 350°F. Oil a large baking sheet or mist it well with nonstick cooking spray. Alternatively, line it with parchment paper or nonstick foil for easiest cleanup.

Combine tofu, mayonnaise, cornmeal, flour, and seasonings in a large bowl. Mix thoroughly into a smooth, thick paste. Add spinach and Parmezano Sprinkles and mix well until evenly distributed. Mixture will be stiff. Form into balls using 2 level tablespoons of the mixture for each. Place on prepared baking sheet. Bake until firm and lightly browned, about 35 to 40 minutes.

QUICHES, DINNER PIES, CASSEROLES, AND SOUFFLÉS

There is something extraordinary about dinner pies and casseroles piping hot from the oven—they make us feel comforted, loved, and satisfied. Whenever they are prepared for us, we know the cook has taken extra care and planning with our meal.

Fortunately, most baked main dishes aren't time-consuming or overly complex to prepare. In this section, you'll find many popular favorites from the original *Uncheese Cookbook*, along with several new recipes and novel variations. Because these dishes are warm and homey, they make wonderful special occasion and company fare as well as everyday delights. There's nothing more appetizing than a steaming hot casserole or dinner pie as the showpiece of a meal.

Important Note for Gluten–Intolerant Individuals:

If you cannot have wheat or gluten, use gluten-free pasta (such as rice, corn, or quinoa pasta) instead of wheat pasta, and always use a gluten-free flour (such as chickpea or rice flour) whenever an option is provided. For recipes that call for a prepared pie crust but do not specify a particular type, feel free to use your favorite gluten-free crust. If no other gluten-containing ingredients are included in the recipe, it will be marked gluten-free.

This simple quiche is easily adapted to a number of variations. It contains no eggs, cream, cow's milk, or cheese, yet it's very creamy and rich tasting.

Classic Quiche

1 prepared 10-inch pie crust

3 cups (about 24 ounces) mashed firm silken tofu, or 3 cups
    drained cooked or canned white beans (two 15-ounce cans)

¾ cup plain nondairy milk or water

½ cup flour (any kind; your choice)

¼ cup nutritional yeast flakes

1 teaspoon salt

¼ teaspoon grated nutmeg

Scant ¼ teaspoon turmeric

⅛ teaspoon white pepper (optional)

1 tablespoon olive or organic canola or safflower oil

1½ cups finely chopped onions

Preheat oven to 400°F. Prebake pie crust 10 to 12 minutes. Let cool. Reduce oven temperature to 350°F. Place tofu or beans, milk or water, flour, nutritional yeast flakes, salt, nutmeg, turmeric, and pepper, if using, in a blender or food processor and process several minutes until mixture is completely smooth. Stop machine frequently to stir mixture and scrape down the sides of the container with a rubber spatula. Set aside.

Heat oil in a medium skillet over medium–high. When hot, add onion and sauté until tender and golden, about 8 minutes. Stir into blended mixture and pour into prepared pie crust. Bake on center rack of oven until top is firm, browned, and slightly puffed, about 40 to 45 minutes. Let rest 15 minutes before slicing.

Per serving:	
calories	342
protein	17 g
fat	18 g
carbohydrate	31 g
calcium	58 mg
sodium	574 mg

FREE
OF:
GLUTEN
SOY
NUTS
CORN

Classic Quiche with "Bacon": Decrease salt to ½ tea-spoon and stir ½ to ⅓ cup vegetarian bacon bits or chopped veggie Canadian bacon into the blended mixture just before pouring into the pie crust. Bake as directed.

Broccoli Quiche: Steam 2 cups bite-size broccoli florets until tender-crisp. Then stir them into the blended mixture just before pouring into the pie crust. Bake as directed.

Spinach Quiche: Cook one 10-ounce package frozen chopped spinach according to package directions. Drain well in a wire mesh strainer, pressing firmly with the back of a wooden spoon, or squeeze it with your hands to express as much liquid as possible. Stir into the blended mixture just before pouring into the pie crust. Bake as directed.

Mushroom Quiche: Add 2 cups sliced mushrooms to the onions once they are soft, and continue sautéing until mush-rooms are tender and almost all of the liquid has evaporated. Stir into the blended mixture just before pouring into the pie crust. Bake as directed.

Squash Quiche: Omit nutmeg. Add 2 cups diced zucchini or yellow summer squash to the onions once they are soft, and continue sautéing until squash is tender. Fold into blend-ed mixture along with 2 teaspoons dried basil just before pouring into the pie crust. Bake as directed.

Scallion Quiche: Omit onions and oil. Stir ½ to 1 cup thinly sliced scallions or chives into the blended mixture just before pouring into the pie crust. Bake as directed. This vari-ation may be used in combination with any of the other variations listed above.

This is a good dish to prepare when you have a bit of extra time because it has a number of steps. However, if the Tofu Ricotta and Parmezano Sprinkles are made in advance, the final assembly is quite speedy.

Per serving:	
calories	356
protein	20 g
fat	11 g
carbohydrate	51 g
calcium	133 mg
sodium	608 mg

FREE OF:
GLUTEN
NUTS
CORN

Three-Cheez Lasagne

1 cup water

⅓ cup nutritional yeast flakes

¼ cup fresh lemon juice

3 to 4 tablespoons sesame tahini

3 tablespoons rolled oats or flour (any kind; your choice)

2 tablespoons kuzu, arrowroot, or cornstarch

2 teaspoons onion powder

½ teaspoon salt

15 lasagna noodles

6 cups seasoned tomato sauce (any kind; your favorite)

½ cup Parmezano Sprinkles, page 50

5 cups Tofu Ricotta (double recipe), page 46

Preheat oven to 350°F. Oil a 9"x13" pan or mist it with non-stick cooking spray. Combine water, nutritional yeast flakes, lemon juice, tahini, oats or flour, kuzu or arrowroot, onion powder, and salt in a blender and process until completely smooth. Set aside.

Cook lasagna noodles according to package directions. Drain, rinse with cold water, and drain again. Place 1 cup of the tomato sauce over bottom of the prepared pan. Arrange a layer of 5 of the lasagna noodles, slightly overlapping them. Spread with one half of the Tofu Ricotta. Drizzle on one third of the blended cheez sauce. Then layer 5 more of the noodles. Top with one half of the remaining tomato sauce. Layer on the remaining half of the Tofu Ricotta and another third of the blended cheez sauce. Top with remaining 5 noodles and the rest of the tomato sauce.

Drizzle top with the remaining blended cheez sauce, and sprinkle with Parmezano Sprinkles.

Bake 45 minutes. If some of the ingredients were prepared in advance and are cold, add 5 to 10 minutes to the baking time. Let stand 10 minutes before serving.

Three Cheez and Spinach Lasagne

Thaw 2 (10-ounce) packages of frozen chopped spinach. Squeeze out as much moisture as possible using your hands, and stir into the Tofu Ricotta before assembling lasagne.

Florentine Ricotta Pie

1 prepared 10-inch pie crust

2 (10 ounce) packages frozen chopped spinach, thawed

½ pound (8 ounces) mashed firm regular tofu,
   or 1 cup drained cooked or canned white beans

1 cup thinly sliced scallions

1 teaspoon dried basil

½ teaspoon dried marjoram

1½ cups water

⅓ cup rolled oats, or ¼ cup flour (any kind; your choice)

⅓ cup nutritional yeast flakes

¼ cup sesame tahini

¼ cup fresh lemon juice

3 tablespoons kuzu, arrowroot, or cornstarch

1¼ teaspoons salt

1 teaspoon onion powder

½ teaspoon dry mustard

Preheat oven to 400°F. Prebake pie crust until lightly golden brown, about 10 to 12 minutes. Let cool. Reduce oven temperature to 350°F.

Place thawed spinach in a mesh strainer, and press or squeeze with your hands to remove as much moisture as possible. Transfer to a bowl and stir in mashed tofu or beans, scallions, basil, and marjoram. Mix well, and set aside.

Combine remaining ingredients in a blender, and process several minutes until very smooth. Pour over spinach and mix thoroughly. Spoon into cooled crust, and bake until the center is firm and the crust is golden brown, about 40 to 50 minutes. Cool 15 minutes. Serve warm or at room temperature. Leftovers are also delicious cold the following day.

Per serving:

calories	266
protein	13 g
fat	15 g
carbohydrate	26 g
calcium	211 mg
sodium	529 mg

FREE OF:
GLUTEN
SOY
NUTS
CORN

Contains sesame tahini.

Frittata

¼ cup water

½ teaspoon crushed garlic

1 medium onion chopped

1 large potato, peeled and diced

1 large green bell pepper, finely diced

1 pound firm regular tofu, crumbled, or 2 cups drained canned
   or cooked white beans (one 15- or 16-ounce can)

1 (16-ounce) can unsalted diced tomatoes, with juice

⅓ cup flour (any kind; your choice)

1 tablespoon kuzu, arrowroot, or cornstarch

1 tablespoon nutritional yeast flakes

1 teaspoon salt

½ teaspoon dried oregano

¼ teaspoon turmeric

⅛ teaspoon pepper

Somewhere between a baked Western cheese omelet and an Italian-style, crustless quiche, this delicious, egg-free frittata is creamy, custardy, and chock-full of potatoes, onions, and peppers. Scoop it onto warm plates, and serve it with toast for a soothing breakfast, brunch, or light supper.

Preheat oven to 350°F. Oil two 10-inch pie plates or mist them with nonstick cooking spray.

Heat water in a medium skillet. Add garlic and stir. Then add onion, potato, and green pepper. Cover and cook, stirring occasionally, until potato is tender, about 10 minutes.

Place remaining ingredients in blender, and process several minutes until velvety smooth. Transfer to a bowl. Stir in cooked vegetables, and mix well. Pour evenly into prepared pie plates, and bake 45 to 50 minutes. Let rest 10 to 15 minutes before serving. Serve hot or warm.

Variation: For a richer version, sauté vegetables in 2 tablespoons olive oil and omit water.

FREE OF:
GLUTEN
SOY
NUTS
CORN

Per serving:	
calories	198
protein	15 g
fat	1 g
carbohydrate	23 g
calcium	185 mg
sodium	379 mg

MAKES 4 TO 6 SERVINGS

This strudel consists of a phyllo dough crust filled with broccoli, onions, and seasoned tofu "cheese." It's elegant enough for company, yet simple enough for everyday fare.

Broccoli Strudel

6 sheets phyllo dough, thawed if frozen

1 tablespoon olive oil

1 ½ cups chopped onions

1 teaspoon crushed garlic

2 cups bite-size broccoli florets

1 pound firm regular tofu, rinsed, patted dry, and finely
   crumbled or mashed

2 tablespoons tamari

2 teaspoons dried oregano

½ teaspoon grated nutmeg

Preheat oven to 350°F. Mist an 8-inch square glass baking pan with nonstick cooking spray, and set aside. Cover phyllo dough with a clean, damp kitchen towel and plastic wrap to prevent it from drying out. Heat oil in a large skillet. When hot, add onions and garlic and sauté until onion is translucent, about 5 minutes. Add broccoli, and continue to sauté until broccoli is bright green and tender–crisp, about 8 to 10 minutes longer. Transfer mixture to a large bowl. Add tofu, tamari, oregano, and nutmeg, and mix well. Arrange half of the phyllo sheets in the prepared baking dish, easing them in gently. Let edges of the dough hang over the sides of the dish. Spoon broccoli–tofu mixture into the phyllo dough, pressing it in gently to make a smooth, even layer. Separate remaining sheets of phyllo dough. Place them, one at a time, on top of the broccoli–tofu mixture. Lightly mist each one with olive oil or nonstick cooking spray. Fold edges of phyllo dough in, and mist top with a little more oil or cooking spray. Bake until crust is golden brown, about 25 to 30 minutes.

Per serving:

calories	260
protein	19 g
fat	11 g
carbohydrate	27 g
calcium	232 mg
sodium	516 mg

FREE OF:
NUTS
YEAST
CORN

Eggplant Parmezano

1 medium eggplant, unpeeled, sliced into ½-inch rounds

2 ripe tomatoes, thinly sliced

½ cup water

¼ cup nutritional yeast flakes

2 tablespoons fresh lemon juice

2 tablespoons sesame tahini

2 tablespoons rolled oats or flour (any kind; your choice)

1 tablespoon kuzu, arrowroot, or cornstarch

1 teaspoon onion powder

¼ teaspoon salt

½ cup Parmezano Sprinkles, page 50,
   or soy-based vegan parmesan alternative

Preheat broiler. Place eggplant slices on a dry baking sheet. Broil 5 inches from heat source for about 5 minutes. Turn over and continue broiling until fork tender, only about 2 minutes longer. Transfer to an oiled baking dish that is large enough to fit the eggplant in a single layer. Top with tomato slices.

Preheat oven to 400°F. Combine remaining ingredients, except Parmezano Sprinkles, in a blender, and process until sauce is completely smooth. Pour over eggplant and tomatoes. Sprinkle top evenly with Parmezano Sprinkles. Bake until golden brown and bubbly, about 20 to 30 minutes.

MAKES 4 SERVINGS

In this recipe the eggplant is broiled instead of breaded and deep fried. Then it is topped with fresh tomato slices and a creamy, mozzarella-style cheez sauce.

FREE OF:
GLUTEN
SOY
NUTS
CORN

Per serving:	
calories	177
protein	10 g
fat	10 g
carbohydrate	18 g
calcium	71 mg
sodium	244 mg

Contains sesame tahini.

When you want to impress your family or company, this is the dish to make.

Per serving:	
calories	234
protein	11 g
fat	15 g
carbohydrate	17 g
calcium	130 mg
sodium	537 mg

FREE OF:
GLUTEN
NUTS
YEAST
CORN

Mediterranean Stuffed Eggplants

3 (½-pound) eggplants

1 teaspoon salt

3 to 4 tablespoons olive oil

2 cups chopped onions

½ teaspoon crushed garlic

½ cup minced fresh parsley

¼ cup minced fresh mint, or 1 tablespoon dried mint

3 Roma tomatoes, halved lengthwise, seeded, and cut into julienne strips

1 cup drained Betta Feta, page 45, coarsely crumbled

Salt and pepper, to taste

Halve 2 eggplants lengthwise and score the pulp deeply with a sharp knife, taking care not to pierce the skins. Using a grape-fruit knife, carefully scoop out pulp and set aside, leaving ½-inch–thick shells. Lightly sprinkle shells with some of the salt and invert on paper towels to drain for 30 minutes. Cut reserved pulp and remaining whole eggplant into ½-inch pieces. Place in a colander and toss with the remaining salt. Let drain in sink 30 minutes.

Pat shells dry with paper towels or a clean kitchen towel, and rub the inside with 1 tablespoon of oil. Alternatively, mist with olive oil spray. Preheat broiler, and broil shells on the rack of a broiler pan, about 4 inches from the heat source, until tender, about 5 minutes.

Pat eggplant pieces dry. Place remaining oil in a large skillet and heat over medium–high. When hot, add eggplant pieces and sauté until golden. Stir in onion and garlic and cook and stir

666

66666666

6666666666

over medium heat until onion is limp and tender. Remove skillet from heat, and stir in parsley, mint, tomatoes, Betta Feta, and salt and pepper to taste. Divide mixture equally between the shells, mounding it. Broil the stuffed eggplants in a large, flameproof baking dish until filling is bubbling and golden, about 5 minutes.

Cheezy Rice and Broccoli Casserole

MAKES 4 SERVINGS

You'll want to make this casserole often, as it is yummy and easy. Everything is mixed directly in the casserole dish, so even cleanup is a breeze.

1 cup uncooked white basmati rice

2 cups plain nondairy milk

½ cup nutritional yeast flakes

2 to 4 tablespoons umeboshi vinegar and/or salt to taste

1 to 2 tablespoons olive oil (optional)

1 teaspoon crushed garlic

1½ to 2 cups fresh or frozen bite-size broccoli florets

Preheat oven to 375°F. Place all ingredients in a 4-quart casserole dish, and mix until well combined. Cover and bake 50 to 60 minutes. Serve hot.

Variation: For a richer yellow color, add ¼ teaspoon turmeric to the mixture prior to baking.

FREE OF:
GLUTEN
SOY
NUTS
CORN

Per serving:
calories 225
protein 15 g
fat 4 g
carbohydrate 38 g
calcium 49 mg
sodium 34 mg

MAKES 4 TO 6 SERVINGS

Pasta tubes known as macaroni came from Italy more than two hundred years ago, but baking them with a cheese sauce didn't become popular in America until the nineteenth century. This cheeseless version has captured the rich taste and tang of traditional macaroni and cheese, yet it's totally dairy-free.

See photo, facing p. 96

Per serving:	
calories	334
protein	16 g
fat	8 g
carbohydrate	50 g
calcium	20 mg
sodium	18 mg

FREE OF:
GLUTEN
SOY
NUTS
CORN

Traditional Macaroni and Cheez

2½ cups dry elbow macaroni

2 tablespoons olive oil

⅓ cup flour (any kind; your choice)

½ teaspoon dry mustard

Pinch of cayenne

1¾ cups plain nondairy milk, heated

½ cup nutritional yeast flakes

Salt and pepper

½ cup packed whole-grain bread crumbs (optional)

Preheat oven to 375°F. Oil an 8–inch square baking dish or mist it with nonstick cooking spray and set aside. Cook macaroni according to package directions. Drain well and set aside.

While macaroni is cooking, prepare cheez sauce. Heat oil in a large saucepan. When hot, stir in flour, mustard, and cayenne. Cook and stir 1 minute. Gradually stir in hot milk, a little at a time, whisking constantly. (It will take about 5 to 7 minutes to add the milk. The sauce should continue to bubble as you add the milk; if it doesn't, you are adding the milk too quickly.) If necessary, cook the sauce until it is the consistency of thick cream, about 2 to 4 minutes longer. Remove from heat and stir in nutritional yeast flakes. Season with salt and pepper to taste. Stir in cooked macaroni, and mix well.

Transfer to the prepared baking dish. Sprinkle bread crumbs, if using, evenly over top. Bake 25 to 30 minutes. Let stand for 5 minutes before serving.

Baked Macaroni and Cheez

2 tablespoons olive or organic canola or safflower oil

1 large onion, finely chopped

4 cups (16 ounces) dry macaroni or other tube pasta (such as penne or ziti)

2 cups water

½ cup roasted red peppers (skin and seeds removed) or pimiento pieces

½ cup raw cashews, or ⅓ cup cashew butter

⅓ cup fresh lemon juice

⅓ cup nutritional yeast flakes

¼ cup nonalcoholic white wine

2 teaspoons onion powder

2 teaspoons garlic powder

1 teaspoon salt

Preheat oven to 350°F. Oil a 3-quart casserole dish or mist it with nonstick cooking spray and set aside. (Alternatively, use a nonstick casserole dish.)

Heat oil in a large saucepan. When hot, add onion and sauté until tender and lightly browned, about 15 to 20 minutes. Meanwhile, cook macaroni according to package directions. Drain well and stir into cooked onions. Mix well.

Combine remaining ingredients in a blender, and process several minutes until completely smooth. Stir into macaroni and onions and then spoon into prepared casserole dish. Bake uncovered 25 to 35 minutes. Serve at once.

MAKES 8 SERVINGS

This version of the popular American standard is just as spectacular as its dairy counterpart—possibly even better, since it has no cholesterol! This recipe is reminiscent of old-fashioned "cafeteria style" macaroni and cheese. As it bakes, the "cheese" forms tiny curds around the pasta, giving it a dry rather than creamy consistency. So if you grew up eating the instant-mix stuff in the blue box, please adjust your expectations! This version may be a little different from what you are accustomed to, but give it a chance—it truly is delicious.

FREE OF:
GLUTEN
SOY
CORN

Per serving:	
calories	310
protein	11 g
fat	9 g
carbohydrate	47 g
calcium	23 mg
sodium	274 mg

MAKES 16 STUFFED
SHELLS (8 SERVINGS)

When you serve these pasta shells—brimming with nondairy ricotta, smothered in a savory marinara sauce, and topped with Parmezano Sprinkles—who could resist?

Baked Stuffed Shells

16 jumbo pasta stuffing shells

6 cups tomato sauce (your favorite)

½ cup Parmezano Sprinkles, page 50,
   or soy-based vegan Parmesan alternative

1 pound firm regular tofu, mashed

⅔ cup vegan mayonnaise

1½ tablespoons minced fresh parsley,
   or 2 teaspoons dried parsley flakes

2 teaspoons dried basil

2 teaspoons onion powder

1 teaspoon garlic powder

Salt and pepper

Preheat oven to 350°F. Oil a 9″ x 13″ baking dish or mist it with nonstick cooking spray. Cook pasta shells according to package directions. Drain well.

In a large bowl, combine tofu, mayonnaise, herbs, and seasonings, and mash into a finely grained paste. Stuff about 2 rounded tablespoonfuls into each shell. Spread a cup or so of tomato sauce over the bottom of the prepared baking dish. Arrange stuffed shells in a single layer over sauce. Spoon remaining sauce over the shells and sprinkle with Parmezano Sprinkles. Bake until heated through, about 30 to 45 minutes.

Per serving:

calories	323
protein	17 g
fat	13 g
carbohydrate	37 g
calcium	132 mg
sodium	631 mg

FREE
OF:
GLUTEN
NUTS
CORN

Lokshen Kugel with Cheez (Creamy Noodle Pudding)

MAKES 6 TO 8 SERVINGS

12 ounces egg-free, wide noodles

1 tablespoon organic canola or safflower oil

2½ to 3 cups Sour Dressing, p. 151

½ pound firm regular tofu, mashed

Salt

Good pinch of grated nutmeg (optional)

Traditionally, noodle kugel contains creamed cottage cheese or pot cheese (a dry curd cottage cheese), sour cream, eggs, butter, and wide egg noodles. This luscious rendition captures all the time-honored flavor without the heavy dairy products and eggs.

Preheat oven to 350°F. Cook noodles according to package directions. Drain well. Transfer to a large bowl and toss with the oil. Combine remaining ingredients in a separate bowl and season with salt and nutmeg, if using. Add to cooked noodles and mix well. Oil a casserole dish large enough to hold noodle mixture. Pour noodle mixture into prepared casserole dish and bake uncovered until firm and golden brown on top, about 30 minutes. Serve hot or cold cut into squares.

Sweet Dessert Kugel

Omit the nutmeg. Add ½ cup sugar, the grated zest of an orange or a lemon, and ½ cup golden or black raisins or dried cherries.

FREE OF:
GLUTEN
NUTS
YEAST
CORN

Per serving:	
calories	245
protein	13 g
fat	13 g
carbohydrate	21 g
calcium	69 mg
sodium	268 mg

**MAKES ABOUT 9
SERVINGS**

Noodle pudding is a
unique food—a main-
dish casserole that is
slightly sweet but often
served with savory foods
accompanying it. Sweet
Noodle Pudding can also
be served for dessert
topped with canned or
fresh fruit or berries.

Sweet Noodle Pudding

1 pound egg-free, wide noodles

1 tablespoon organic canola or safflower oil

1 pound firm regular tofu, mashed

1½ cups Sour Dressing, page 151

½ cup seedless raisins

⅓ cup pure maple syrup

1¼ teaspoons salt

1 teaspoon ground cinnamon

½ cup ground pecans

Preheat oven to 350°F. Cook noodles according to package
directions. Drain well. Transfer to a large bowl and toss with the
oil. Combine tofu, Sour Dressing, raisins, maple syrup, salt, and
cinnamon in a separate bowl. Add to cooked noodles and mix
well. Pack into an oiled or nonstick 8″ x 8″ pan (or mist pan with
nonstick cooking spray), distributing mixture evenly. Sprinkle
ground pecans evenly over the top. Bake uncovered 25 to 30
minutes. Serve hot, warm, or cold cut into squares.

Variations

• For variety, add a pinch of ground allspice, coriander, cardamom, ginger, or nutmeg along with the cinnamon.

• Add chopped dried apricots or prunes along with or instead
of the raisins.

Per serving:

calories	312
protein	14 g
fat	15 g
carbohydrate	6 g
calcium	133 mg
sodium	539 mg

**FREE
OF:
GLUTEN
YEAST
CORN**

Spinach-Tofu Manicotti

MAKES ABOUT 12 MANICOTTI

This is a hearty dish that is great for family dinners while still being elegant enough for guests.

12 manicotti tubes

1 pound firm regular tofu, mashed

1 (10 ounce) package frozen chopped spinach, thawed and squeezed dry

½ cup vegan mayonnaise

2 teaspoons onion powder

1 teaspoon garlic powder

1 teaspoon each: dried basil, oregano, and marjoram

½ pound (8 ounces) mushrooms, chopped

Salt, pepper, and crushed red pepper flakes

4 cups (32 ounces) tomato sauce (your favorite)

Parmezano Sprinkles, page 50, or soy-based vegan parmesan alternative (optional)

Preheat oven to 350°F. Oil a large shallow baking dish (large enough to fit 12 stuffed manicotti shells) or mist it with nonstick cooking spray. Cook manicotti according to package directions. Drain well and set aside. In a large bowl, combine tofu, mayonnaise, spinach, onion and garlic powders, and herbs until evenly blended. Stir in mushrooms. Season with salt, pepper, and crushed red pepper flakes to taste. Using a spoon or your fingers, stuff tofu mixture equally into manicotti tubes.

Spread a thin layer of tomato sauce over the bottom of the prepared baking dish. Arrange stuffed manicotti shells in a single layer over sauce. Pour remaining sauce evenly over manicotti. Cover dish with a lid or foil and bake until hot and bubbly, about 45 to 50 minutes. Let stand 10 minutes before serving. Pass Parmezano Sprinkles at the table, if desired.

FREE OF:
NUTS
YEAST
CORN

Per manicotti:	
calories	221
protein	12 g
fat	7 g
carbohydrate	30 g
calcium	114 mg
sodium	295 mg

Light, cheesy, and "eggy" blintzes without the eggs or cheese are spectacular! Top them with a dab of fruit-sweetened jam, or a spoonful of Sour Dressing, page 151, or unsweetened applesauce for a truly authentic flavor.

Per serving:	
calories	264
protein	19 g
fat	8 g
carbohydrate	35 g
calcium	109 mg
sodium	663 mg

FREE OF:
GLUTEN
NUTS
YEAST
CORN

Blintzes

2 cups chickpea flour

½ teaspoon salt

¼ teaspoon turmeric

2½ cups water

1 pound firm regular tofu, rinsed, drained, and mashed

½ cup mashed firm silken tofu

2 tablespoons fresh lemon juice

1 to 2 tablespoons sweetener of your choice

1 teaspoon vanilla extract

1 teaspoon salt

½ teaspoon cinnamon

To make the blintz wrappers, combine chickpea flour, salt, and turmeric in a medium bowl. Gradually stir in water beating with a fork or wire whisk. Go slowly in order to avoid lumps. Let the batter rest 15 minutes. To make the filling, combine both kinds of tofu, lemon juice, sweetener, vanilla, salt, and cinnamon in a large bowl. Mash together into a smooth, finely grained paste. Alternatively, ingredients may be blended in a food processor for a smoother texture. Set aside.

Preheat oven to 350°F. Lightly oil a 10-inch nonstick skillet or crêpe pan, and heat over medium-high. (A nonstick pan will work best.) When the skillet is very hot (when water dropped on it beads and dances across the surface), pour on the batter using a scant ¼ cup for each wrapper. Immediately swirl it into a very thin circle, about 5 to 6 inches in diameter. Cook until the top surface appears dry and the bottom has some nicely browned spots. Carefully loosen and turn over wrapper. Cook the second side briefly, just until very lightly flecked with brown. Stack on a place while remainder cook. Re-oil pan as necessary.

To assemble the blintzes, spread about 2 slightly rounded tablespoonfuls of filling on each wrapper, placing it in a horizontal line about 1 inch from the edge nearest to you. Fold in left and right sides about 1 inch. Then gently roll wrapper into a neat packet, starting with the end with the filling. Alternatively, just gently roll wrapper around filling without folding in the sides. Arrange blintzes on a lightly oiled or nonstick baking sheet. Alternatively, use a baking sheet misted with nonstick cooking spray or lined with parchment paper or nonstick foil. Bake until the filling is heated through, about 10 minutes. Serve at once.

Tip: Store any leftover filling in the refrigerator. It will keep for about 4 days.

MAKES 6 SERVINGS

Tetrazzini is a main dish casserole that typically includes cooked chicken, turkey, or fish; pasta; mushrooms; and sometimes almonds in a rich cream sauce topped with Parmesan cheese. With a few adaptations, we've created a fabulous, healthful, vegan version.

Per serving:	
calories	442
protein	20 g
fat	15 g
carbohydrate	61 g
calcium	69 mg
sodium	298 mg

FREE OF:
GLUTEN SOY NUTS YEAST CORN

Tetrazzini

1 pound spaghetti, broken in half

2 tablespoons olive oil

4 cups (about 12 ounces) thinly sliced fresh mushrooms

1 red bell pepper, finely diced

1 cup flour (any kind; your choice)

4 cups plain nondairy milk

½ cup nutritional yeast flakes (optional)

1 tablespoon onion powder

1 teaspoon garlic powder

½ teaspoon salt

1 cup frozen green peas, thawed

½ to 1 cup Parmezano Sprinkles, page 50,
    or soy-based vegan parmesan alternative

Protein or vegetable options (choose one)

1¾ cups drained cooked or canned chickpeas (one 15- or 16-ounce can)

½ pound (8 ounces) seasoned or smoked tofu cut in ¼-inch cubes

½ pound (8 ounces) cubed tempeh

2 cups cooked asparagus cut in 1-inch lengths

2 cups chicken-style seitan cut in 1-inch chunks

Preheat oven to 350°F. Oil a shallow, 4–quart casserole dish or mist it with nonstick cooking spray. Set aside.

Cook spaghetti according to package directions. Drain and place in a large bowl. Meanwhile, heat oil in a large saucepan. Add mushrooms and bell pepper, and sauté until tender.

Combine flour, half the milk, and all of the seasonings in a blender and process until smooth. Pour over cooked mushrooms and pepper along with remaining milk. Mix well, and cook and stir until slightly thickened and bubbly. Remove from heat and stir in peas. Pour over pasta, add chickpeas (or other option of your choice), and toss gently. Spoon into prepared casserole dish and dust the top with Parmezano Sprinkles. Bake until hot, bubbly, and golden brown on top, about 30 to 35 minutes. Serve at once.

Tomato and Cheez Soufflé

1½ cups water

½ cup roasted red peppers (skin and seeds removed) or pimiento pieces

½ cup raw cashews, or ⅓ cup cashew butter

3 tablespoons nutritional yeast flakes

3 tablespoons fresh lemon juice

2 tablespoons nonalcoholic white wine (optional)

1½ teaspoons onion powder

1¼ teaspoons salt

½ teaspoon dry mustard

½ teaspoon dried thyme

½ teaspoon garlic powder

Pepper

6 to 9 slices whole-grain or rice bread (crusts may be removed, if desired)

3 ripe tomatoes, sliced

Preheat oven to 375°F. Oil a 2-quart baking dish or soufflé dish or mist it with nonstick cooking spray. Place all ingredients, except bread and tomatoes, in a blender and process several minutes until completely smooth. Place a layer of 2 to 3 slices of bread in the bottom of the prepared baking dish, followed by a layer of tomatoes and one third of the blended sauce, then another layer of bread and tomatoes, followed by half of the remaining sauce. Finish with a final layer of bread and tomatoes, followed by the remainder of the sauce. Bake until lightly puffed and golden brown, about 45 to 50 minutes. Serve at once.

MAKES 6 SERVINGS

Here's a simple, luscious casserole for busy nights or whenever you're in the mood for something decadently cheezy.

FREE OF:
GLUTEN
SOY
CORN

Per serving:	
calories	176
protein	7 g
fat	9 g
carbohydrate	21 g
calcium	38 mg
sodium	584 mg

Here is a classic and appealing way to get your greens. Spinach has never been more appetizing!

Spinach and Cheez Soufflé

1½ cups water

1 (10-ounce) package frozen chopped spinach, thawed and squeezed dry

½ cup roasted red peppers (skin and seeds removed) or pimiento pieces

½ cup raw cashews, or ⅓ cup cashew butter

¼ cup nonalcoholic white wine

3 tablespoons nutritional yeast flakes

3 tablespoons fresh lemon juice

1½ teaspoons onion powder

1¼ teaspoons salt

½ teaspoon dry mustard

½ teaspoon dried thyme

½ teaspoon garlic powder

Pepper

6 to 9 slices whole-grain or rice bread (crusts may be removed, if desired)

Preheat oven to 375°F. Oil a 2-quart baking dish or soufflé dish or mist it with nonstick cooking spray. Place all ingredients, except bread, in a blender and process several minutes until completely smooth. Place a layer of 2 to 3 slices of bread in the bottom of the prepared baking dish, followed by a layer of one third of the blended sauce, then another layer of bread, followed by half of the remaining sauce. Finish with a final layer of bread, followed by the remainder of the sauce. Bake until lightly puffed and golden brown, about 45 to 50 minutes. Serve at once.

Per serving:	
calories	183
protein	8 g
fat	9 g
carbohydrate	20 g
calcium	105 mg
sodium	620 mg

FREE OF:
GLUTEN
SOY
CORN

PIZZAS, BREADS, LITTLE BITES, AND SANDWICHES

In this chapter, you'll find an assortment of inspired pizzas and home-made breads—some traditional, some contemporary, some avant-garde—all tasty and dairy free. Once you try the recipes as written, feel free to experiment by incorporating some of the ideas below. You're certain to come up with your own signature pizza or bread to wow your friends and family.

Pizza Pizzazz

Can pizza still be pizza without the cheese? Of course! There are countless alternatives to cheese that add richness and a lively jolt of flavor. Pizza toppings are limited only by your imagination. Here are just a few ideas:

- artichoke hearts, canned or marinated
- arugula
- baba ghanoush
- basil, fresh
- bean dip
- beans, whole, mashed, or refried
- broccoli, minced or bite-size florets
- capers
- carrots, shredded
- corn
- eggplant, grilled or roasted
- garlic, roasted or sliced fresh
- hearts of palm
- hummus
- mock meats (veggie burger crumbles, veggie bacon, veggie pepperoni or salami)
- mushrooms, thinly sliced
- nutritional yeast
- olives, sliced (black, green, oil cured, stuffed)
- onions (red, white, or yellow), chopped or thinly sliced
- Parmezano Sprinkles (recipe page 50), or soy-based vegan parmesan alternative

- peppers (sweet bell, hot, raw, roasted), sliced, diced, or chopped
- pesto (see recipe on page 44)
- pineapple tidbits
- salsa
- scallions, sliced
- shallots, minced
- spinach, raw or well-drained cooked
- tempeh, cubed or grated
- texturized vegetable protein, reconstituted
- tofu, seasoned or smoked, crumbled or finely diced
- tomatoes, chopped sundried
- tomatoes, crushed, seasoned with fresh or dried herbs
- tomatoes, fresh Roma
- tomato sauce
- uncheese sauces (see recipes on pages 53 to 70), drizzled
- uncheeses, block-style (see recipes on pages 157 to 166), finely diced or gently grated
- veggies, minced raw, drizzled with olive oil
- zucchini, sliced or diced

Contemporary Crusts

Pizza crusts can be as varied as your toppings. Traditional pizza dough notwithstanding, here is a sampling of some of the many other creative possibilities:

- bagels
- chapatis
- cornbread
- English muffins
- focaccia
- French baguettes
- Italian bread
- lavash
- pita bread
- polenta (corn or rice)
- rolls, Kaiser
- tortillas, corn or whole wheat

Sandwiches

What exactly is a sandwich? Basically anything on a slice of bread. Indeed, a sandwich doesn't even require two slices of bread, because there are "open-face" sandwiches, too. To complicate matters, there are double- and triple-decker versions as well, and these have three or four bread slices layered and stacked among various fillings. And we wouldn't want to overlook the submarine sandwich (also known as a "hero" or "grinder," among other names) and the venerable veggie dog and veggie burger on a bun, which certainly hold their own in this category.

Sandwiches usually are eaten out of hand, but extra sloppy or gooey sandwiches may require a knife and fork. Of course, bread these days can suggest anything from the traditional, yeast-risen loaf to pita rounds, flat breads, bagels, and quick breads. Wraps are more popular than ever. These involve a flat bread—such as a tortilla, chapati, or lavash—that is slathered with a spread, covered with chopped veggies, sprouts, beans, tofu, seitan, or other tasty delicacies, and then rolled or folded to enclose the filling. Here are some of the many "bread" and "wrapper" options available for both conventional and unconventional sandwiches:

- bagels
- Indian roti or chapatis
- lavash
- matzos
- rice cakes
- corn cakes
- soft or crusty rolls
- tortillas (flour or corn)
- whole-grain crackers
- whole-grain or multigrain breads
- gluten-free rice bread
- sourdough bread
- sprouted grain bread
- pita bread

In this section we provide a collection of mouth-watering, cheezy sandwiches—some served traditional-style, others served open-face or heated. If you are sensitive to gluten, be sure to use gluten-free rice bread or rolls for sandwiches or corn tortillas for wraps.

Have your pizza just the way you like it—super quick and easy with only the toppings you most enjoy.

Tortilla Pizza Express

1 six-inch tortilla (corn or wheat)

1 tablespoon pizza sauce (your favorite kind)

½ to ⅔ cup finely chopped vegetables (your favorite kinds; see pages 123 to 124 for ideas)

Olive oil spray

Salt

1 to 2 teaspoons Parmezano Sprinkles, page 50, or soy-based vegan parmesan alternative (optional)

Preheat oven to 350°F. Place the tortilla on a baking sheet or broiler pan. Spread sauce evenly over the tortilla. Top carefully with vegetables. Mist with olive oil, and sprinkle with salt to taste. Bake until lightly browned on top and tortilla is crisp, about 15 to 20 minutes. Dust with Parmezano Sprinkles, if desired. Serve hot.

Tips: You can use minced raw vegetables to top your pizza, or, if you prefer, use thicker or larger pieces that have been steamed, roasted, or grilled in advance.

• If your tortilla is larger than six–inches in diameter, increase the amount of sauce and vegetables accordingly.

• This recipe can be doubled, tripled, or quadrupled to accommodate a crowd.

• For a crispier crust, bake the tortilla 5 minutes before adding sauce and toppings.

Per serving:	
calories	115
protein	3 g
fat	2 g
carbohydrate	21 g
calcium	11 mg
sodium	197 mg

FREE OF:
GLUTEN
SOY
NUTS
YEAST
CORN

20-Minute Bean Pizzas

MAKES 2 TORTILLA PIZZAS

Corn tortillas make a quick and easy pizza crust, while beans make a hearty and substantial topping.

2 six-inch corn tortillas

½ cup drained cooked or canned white beans

2 to 3 tablespoons pizza sauce (your favorite kind)

2 to 3 tablespoon Parmezano Sprinkles, page 50, or soy-based vegan parmesan alternative

1 to 2 teaspoons olive oil (optional)

¼ teaspoon dried oregano

¼ teaspoon garlic powder

Pinch each: salt, pepper, and cayenne

Preheat oven to 400°F. Place tortillas on a dry baking sheet. Using a potato masher or fork, mash beans with remaining ingredients. Spread bean mixture evenly over tortillas. Bake until lightly browned on top and tortilla is crisp, about 20 minutes. Serve hot.

FREE OF: GLUTEN SOY NUTS YEAST	Per serving:	
	calories	166
	protein	10 g
	fat	3 g
	carbohydrate	26 g
	calcium	128 mg
	sodium	327 mg

Instant Mini-Pizzas

MAKES 4 MINI PIZZAS

These super-quick pizzas make a terrific snack or light lunch or dinner accompanied by a salad or vegetable.

4 six-inch corn tortillas

½ cup pizza sauce (your favorite kind)

¼ cup cashew butter or sesame tahini

1 to 2 tablespoons nutritional yeast flakes (optional)

Preheat oven to 350°F. Place tortillas on a dry baking sheet. Combine pizza sauce with cashew butter or sesame tahini until completely smooth and creamy. Stir in nutritional yeast flakes, if using. Spread equally and evenly over tortillas. Bake until sauce is hot and tortilla is crisp around the edges, about 15 to 18 minutes. Serve at once.

FREE OF: GLUTEN SOY NUTS YEAST	Per serving:	
	calories	174
	protein	5 g
	fat	10 g
	carbohydrate	18 g
	calcium	27 mg
	sodium	210 mg

Contains sesame tahini.

127

This unusual pizza is simple to prepare and tastes amazing. If you have chickpea flour on hand, it can be on the table in a jiffy.

Chickpea Flour Pizza

½ cup chickpea flour

¼ teaspoon salt

¼ teaspoon dried oregano, crumbled between your fingers

¼ teaspoon dried basil, crumbled between your fingers

¼ teaspoon garlic powder

Generous pinch of cayenne or pepper

Pinch of turmeric

½ cup water

1 teaspoon olive oil

Place chickpea flour, salt, oregano, basil, garlic powder, cayenne, and turmeric in a medium bowl. Gradually whisk in water, beating well after each addition until completely smooth. Generously oil a 10-inch skillet (nonstick will work best) or mist it well with nonstick cooking spray, and heat over medium–high. When hot, stir batter and pour into pan. Drizzle olive oil over top. Cook until top is set and bottom is nicely browned, about 5 to 7 minutes. Adjust heat as necessary. Carefully turn over and cook other side until well browned, about 5 minutes. Slide onto a round plate and slice into 8 wedges. Serve hot.

Per slice:	
calories	30
protein	2 g
fat	1 g
carbohydrate	4 g
calcium	0 mg
sodium	68 mg

FREE OF:
GLUTEN
SOY
NUTS
YEAST
CORN

French Bread Pizza

MAKES 1 PIZZA (ABOUT 4 TO 6 SERVINGS)

1 loaf French bread, cut in half width- and lengthwise

½ pound firm regular tofu, rinsed, drained, and crumbled, or 1½ cups drained cooked or canned white beans (one 15-ounce can)

2 tablespoons tomato paste

2 tablespoons olive oil

1 tablespoon tamari or balsamic vinegar

1 teaspoon ground fennel or dried basil

1 teaspoon dried oregano

1 teaspoon crushed garlic

⅛ to ¼ teaspoon cayenne

Salt and pepper

With this superb, split-second pizza, a delectable tofu pâté sits atop a crunchy French bread crust. Now who said fast food can't be delicious and healthful?

Preheat oven to 450°F. Place bread, cut side up, on a dry baking sheet (or pizza pan or baking stone). Combine remaining ingredients in a food processor fitted with a metal blade and blend into a smooth paste. Spread mixture evenly over bread. Bake until tofu is hot and lightly browned and crust is crisp, about 10 to 15 minutes. Serve hot.

FREE OF:
SOY
NUTS
CORN

Per serving:	
calories	259
protein	12 g
fat	11 g
carbohydrate	29 g
calcium	134 mg
sodium	529 mg

Stuff bread, not birds! That's exactly what you'll do with this tantalizing recipe. The cheezy tofu filling tastes like a rich, well-seasoned ricotta. Serve these scrumptious calzones plain, or, if you prefer, topped with a spoonful or two of pizza sauce. Although the directions may appear lengthy, this is a very simple recipe to prepare.

Per serving:	
calories	110
protein	10 g
fat	6 g
carbohydrate	6 g
calcium	123 mg
sodium	543 mg

FREE OF:
NUTS
CORN

Cheezy Zucchini and Herb Calzones

Dough

1 teaspoon active dry yeast

¾ cup lukewarm water (between 105°F to 115°F)

2 teaspoons sweetener of your choice

½ teaspoon salt

2 to 3 cups whole wheat flour, more or less, as needed

Ricotta–Style Filling

1 teaspoon olive oil

1 cup finely diced zucchini

½ teaspoon crushed garlic

½ pound firm regular tofu, rinsed and patted dry

2 tablespoons minced fresh parsley

1 teaspoon dried basil

½ teaspoon dried oregano

½ teaspoon salt

⅛ teaspoon grated nutmeg

⅛ teaspoon pepper

To make the dough, place yeast in a large bowl, and pour the warm water over it. Let rest 5 minutes. Add sweetener and salt, then, using a wooden spoon, beat in enough flour to make a soft but kneadable dough. Turn dough out onto a floured board, and knead 5 minutes until smooth and elastic. Lightly oil a clean, large bowl, and place dough in it. Turn dough over so it is lightly oiled on all sides. Cover bowl with a clean, damp kitchen towel, and let rise in a warm place for 1 hour.

Meanwhile, heat oil in a 9-inch or 10-inch skillet. When hot, add zucchini and garlic, and sauté until zucchini is just tender, about 3 to 5 minutes.

Place tofu in a medium bowl and mash well. Add parsley, basil, oregano, salt, nutmeg, and pepper and mix well. Fold in cooked zucchini and set aside.

Preheat oven to 400°F. Oil a baking sheet, mist it with nonstick cooking spray, or line it with parchment paper for easiest cleanup, and set aside. Punch down dough and divide into 4 equal balls. Keep dough covered with the same towel that covered the bowl, and work with 1 ball of dough at a time. Place the ball on a lightly floured board and roll into a 6-inch round. Place ¼ of the filling (about ½ cup for each calzone) slightly off the center of the round, and fold the dough over. Seal the edges of the calzone by crimping them with your fingers or with the tines of a fork dipped in flour. Prick the calzones in a few places on top with the tines of the fork. Place them on the prepared baking sheet as soon as they are formed. Mist tops lightly with nonstick cooking spray or olive oil. Bake on the center rack of the oven until lightly browned, about 20 minutes.

Tip: For a lighter tasting crust, substitute unbleached white flour for up to half of the whole wheat flour.

Calzones could be described as individual pizzas with the filling completely enclosed in the crust rather than on top of it. To maximize your time, prepare the filling while the dough is rising. Serve plain or with your favorite marinara or pizza sauce.

Spinach and Cheez Calzones

Dough

1½ teaspoons active dry yeast

1 cup lukewarm water (between 105°F to 115°F)

½ to 1 teaspoon sweetener of your choice

¾ teaspoon salt

2 to 3 cups whole wheat flour, more or less as needed

Spinach and Cheez Filling

1 (10-ounce) package frozen chopped spinach

2 tablespoons olive oil

½ cup chopped onions

1 teaspoon crushed garlic

1 pound firm regular tofu, rinsed, patted dry, and mashed

3 tablespoons fresh lemon juice

2 teaspoons dried basil

1 teaspoon onion powder

½ teaspoon garlic powder

Pinch of each: grated nutmeg and pepper

½ cup Parmezano Sprinkles, page 50, or soy-based
     vegan parmesan alternative

To make the dough, place yeast in a large bowl and pour the warm water over it. Let rest 5 minutes. Add sweetener and salt, then, using a wooden spoon, beat in enough flour to make a soft but kneadable dough. Turn dough out onto a floured board and knead 5 minutes until smooth and elastic. Lightly oil a clean, large bowl and place dough in it. Turn dough over so it is light–ly oiled on all sides. Cover bowl with a clean, damp kitchen towel, and let dough rise in a warm place for 1 hour.

Per serving:	
calories	352
protein	20 g
fat	11 g
carbohydrate	45 g
calcium	224 mg
sodium	483 mg

FREE
OF:
NUTS
CORN

Cook spinach according to package directions. Place in a wire mesh strainer and press firmly with the back of a sturdy spoon or squeeze with your hands to express as much liquid as possible. Set aside. Heat oil in a medium skillet. When hot, add onion and garlic and sauté until onion is just tender, about 10 minutes. Transfer to a large bowl and stir in remaining ingredients, including reserved spinach. Mix thoroughly to distribute all ingredients evenly.

Preheat oven to 400°F. Oil a baking sheet, mist it with nonstick cooking spray, or line it with parchment paper for easiest cleanup, and set aside. Punch down dough and divide into 6 equal balls. Keep dough covered with the same towel that covered the bowl, and work with 1 ball of dough at a time. Place the ball on a lightly floured board and roll into a 6-inch round. Place a heaping ½ cup of filling on one half of the round only. Fold the empty side of the dough over to enclose filling. Seal edges of the calzone by crimping them with your fingers or with the tines of a fork dipped in flour. Prick the calzones in a few places on top with the tines of the fork. Place them on the prepared baking sheet as soon as they are formed. Mist tops lightly with nonstick cooking spray or olive oil. Bake on the center rack of the oven until golden brown, about 20 to 25 minutes.

Tip: For a lighter tasting crust, substitute unbleached white flour for up to half of the whole wheat flour.

Focaccia is a thin, cracker-like Italian bread. This heavenly version is fun to make, and the aroma while it is baking is divine.

Per serving:

calories	235
protein	8 g
fat	6 g
carbohydrate	37 g
calcium	15 mg
sodium	358 mg

FREE OF:
SOY
NUTS
CORN

Sweet Pepper and Onion Focaccia

Dough

1 tablespoon active dry yeast

¾ cup warm water (between 105°F to 115°F)

2 cups whole wheat flour, more or less as needed

1 teaspoon salt

Yellow cornmeal or coarse rice flour

Topping

2 tablespoons olive oil

2 large Vidalia or sweet Spanish onions, sliced

1 (7-ounce) jar roasted red peppers, drained and sliced into strips (remove any skin and seeds)

¾ teaspoon dried rosemary, well crumbled

⅛ teaspoon salt

To make the dough, place yeast in a small bowl and pour the warm water over it. Let rest 5 minutes. Stir in flour and salt to make a soft dough. Turn dough onto a lightly floured surface. Knead until smooth and elastic, about 5 minutes, adding more flour if necessary. Lightly oil a clean, large bowl and place dough in it. Turn dough over so it is oiled on all sides. Cover bowl with a clean, damp kitchen towel, and let the dough rise in a warm place for 1 hour.

While crust is rising, prepare onions. Heat oil in a large skillet over medium–high heat. Add onions and sauté until tender, about 10 minutes. Set aside.

Preheat oven to 425°F. Lightly sprinkle a large baking sheet or jelly–roll pan with cornmeal. Punch down dough. Roll or pat dough into a 13 x 9-inch rectangle on the prepared baking sheet.

Spoon the prepared onions over dough; top with roasted red pepper strips, and sprinkle evenly with rosemary and salt. Bake on the lowest rack of the oven until golden brown, about 20 minutes.

Caramelized Onion, Olive, and Walnut Focaccia

The salty tang of olives and the sharp flavor of walnuts offset the sweetness of the onions in this attention-grabbing recipe.

Dough

1 tablespoon active dry yeast

¾ cup warm water (between 105°F to 115°F)

2 cups whole wheat flour, more or less as needed

1 teaspoon salt

Yellow cornmeal or coarse rice flour

Topping

2 tablespoons olive oil

2 large Vidalia or other sweet onions, sliced

½ cup sliced pitted black or oil-cured olives

½ cup chopped walnuts

1 teaspoon dried oregano

⅛ teaspoon salt

Follow instructions for Sweet Pepper and Onion Focaccia on the facing page.

FREE OF:
SOY
CORN

Per serving:	
calories	311
protein	10 g
fat	14 g
carbohydrate	37 g
calcium	34 mg
sodium	488 mg

Roma tomatoes are thick and meaty. When combined with rosemary and olive oil their flavor is greatly enhanced. For a lower-fat version, omit the olive oil and mist the top of the focaccia well with olive oil spray just before baking.

Per serving:	
calories	225
protein	7 g
fat	9 g
carbohydrate	29 g
calcium	5 mg
sodium	464 mg

FREE OF:
SOY
NUTS
CORN

Tomato and Rosemary Focaccia

Dough

1 tablespoon active dry yeast

¾ cup warm water (between 105°F to 115°F)

2 cups whole wheat flour, more or less as needed

1 teaspoon salt

Yellow cornmeal or coarse rice flour

Topping

4 Roma tomatoes, sliced into ⅛-inch thick rounds

½ teaspoon salt

1 teaspoon dried rosemary, well crumbled

¼ cup olive oil

To make the dough, place yeast in a small bowl and pour the warm water over it. Let rest 5 minutes. Stir in flour and salt to make a soft dough. Turn the dough onto lightly floured surface. Knead until smooth and elastic, about 5 minutes, adding more flour if necessary. Lightly oil a clean, large bowl and place dough in it. Turn dough over so it is oiled on all sides. Cover bowl with a clean, damp kitchen towel and let the dough rise in a warm place for 1 hour.

Preheat oven to 425°F. Lightly sprinkle a large baking sheet or jelly-roll pan with cornmeal. Punch down dough. Roll or pat dough into a 13 x 9-inch rectangle on the prepared baking sheet. Arrange tomato slices in a single layer over the dough and sprinkle evenly with rosemary and salt. Drizzle olive oil evenly over all. Bake on the lowest rack of the oven until golden brown, about 20 minutes.

Tomato and Garlic Focaccia

MAKES 6 SERVINGS

This extraordinary focaccia has a crunchy poppy seed topping.

Dough

1 tablespoon active dry yeast

¾ cup warm water (between 105°F to 115°F)

2 cups whole wheat flour, more or less as needed

1 teaspoon salt

Yellow cornmeal or coarse rice flour

Topping

½ cup tomato juice

1½ tablespoons crushed garlic

1½ teaspoons poppy seeds

¼ teaspoon crushed red pepper flakes or Tabasco

To make the dough, place yeast in a small bowl and pour the warm water over it. Let rest 5 minutes. Stir in flour and salt to make a soft dough. Turn dough onto a lightly floured surface. Knead until smooth and elastic, about 5 minutes, adding more flour if necessary. Lightly oil a clean, large bowl and place dough in it. Turn dough over so it is oiled on all sides. Cover bowl with a clean, damp kitchen towel and let the dough in a warm place for 1 hour.

Preheat oven to 425°F. Lightly sprinkle a large baking sheet or jelly-roll pan with cornmeal. Punch down dough. Roll or pat dough into a 13 x 9-inch rectangle on the prepared baking sheet. Combine topping ingredients in a small bowl and spread over dough to within ½-inch of the edge. Bake on the lowest rack of the oven until golden brown, about 20 minutes.

FREE OF:
SOY
NUTS
CORN

Per serving:	
calories	148
protein	7 g
fat	1 g
carbohydrate	31 g
calcium	27 mg
sodium	431 mg

Salty dill pickles combined with rich tahini and juicy tomatoes make a memorable sandwich more satisfying than cheese. It's also more healthful and exceptionally delicious.

Pickle, Tahini, and Tomato Sandwiches

4 slices whole-grain or gluten-free rice bread,
   toasted if desired

2 tablespoons sesame tahini

2 large leaves romaine or leaf lettuce,
   washed and patted dry

1 medium tomato, thickly sliced

2 thin slices mild red onion (optional)

2 low-sodium dill pickles, thinly sliced lengthwise

Salt and pepper

Spread one side of each slice of bread or toast with some of the tahini. Over two of the slices, layer the pickles, tomato, and onion slices, if using. Sprinkle with salt and pepper to taste. Top with lettuce leaves and remaining bread or toast slices, tahini side in.

Per serving:	
calories	232
protein	8 g
fat	12 g
carbohydrate	28 g
calcium	119 mg
sodium	233 mg

FREE OF:
GLUTEN
SOY
NUTS
CORN

Contains sesame tahini.

Guacamole Grillers

MAKES 2 TO 3 SANDWICHES

Avocado Cheez #1

1 ripe Hass avocado

2 to 4 tablespoons fresh lemon juice

Dash of each: garlic powder and chili powder

Cayenne or Tabasco (optional)

Salt

Avocado Cheez #2

1 ripe Hass avocado

2 to 3 tablespoons nutritional yeast flakes

Crushed garlic or garlic powder (optional)

Several shakes of umeboshi vinegar

Prepare either cheez. Peel avocado and mash well with a fork or potato masher or blend in a food processor fitted with a metal blade for a smoother consistency. Blend in seasonings to taste. Spread equally on two or three slices of bread, and close each sandwich with an additional slice of bread. Oil a skillet or coat it lightly with nonhydrogenated vegan margarine and heat over medium high. Grill both sides of sandwiches until golden brown.

Variations: Add 1 to 2 tablespoons finely minced fresh tomato. Alternatively, add 1 tablespoon minced sundried tomatoes.

• Add 1 to 3 teaspoons well–drained pickle relish.

• Put 1 slice of fresh tomato in each sandwich just prior to grilling.

Well-seasoned avocado makes a delightful replacement for cheese in grilled sandwiches. The smooth richness of the avocado, offset by the tartness of lemon juice or vinegar (which also helps to prevent discoloration), and a pinch of salt and seasonings provide a natural combination of taste sensations commonly associated with aged cheese. Unlike cheese, however, avocados contribute healthful fats and fiber in addition to luscious flavor.

Cheez #1 (no bread)
Per sandwich:

calories	106
protein	1 g
fat	10 g
carbohydrate	5 g
calcium	7 mg
sodium	7 mg

FREE OF:
GLUTEN
SOY
NUTS
CORN

Cheez #2 (no bread)
Per sandwich:

calories	122
protein	5 g
fat	10 g
carbohydrate	6 g
calcium	10 mg
sodium	9 mg

This gorgeous orange cheez makes wonderful, quick grilled sandwiches. Leftover cheez can be stored in the refrigerator for several days, so you can prepare these delicious sandwiches whenever you like!

All American Grilled Cheez

1⅓ cups water

½ cup roasted red peppers (skin and seeds removed) or pimiento pieces

⅓ cup quick-cooking rolled oats

⅓ cup raw cashews

¼ cup nutritional yeast flakes

3 tablespoons fresh lemon juice

2 tablespoons kuzu, arrowroot, or cornstarch

1 tablespoon sesame tahini

2 teaspoons onion powder

1¼ teaspoons salt

¼ teaspoon each: garlic powder, ground dill seed or coriander, dry mustard, and paprika

Pinch of cayenne

16 slices whole-grain or gluten-free rice bread

2 ripe tomatoes, sliced (optional)

Combine all ingredients, except bread and tomatoes, in a blender and process until mixture is completely smooth. Pour into a medium saucepan and bring to a boil stirring constantly. Reduce heat to low and cook, stirring constantly, until mixture is very thick and smooth. Remove from heat. Place 4 of the bread slices on a flat surface. Cover one side of each slice evenly with the cooked mixture. Top with a tomato slice, if desired, and remaining bread slices.

Grill in a large, heavy skillet misted with nonstick cooking spray or coated with a small amount of vegetable oil or nonhy-drogenated vegan margarine. Brown each side well, carefully turning over once. Slice sandwiches in half diagonally, and serve at once.

Per serving:	
calories	200
protein	8 g
fat	8 g
carbohydrate	27 g
calcium	57 mg
sodium	547 mg

FREE OF:
GLUTEN
SOY
CORN

For a gluten-free version, replace the oats with any gluten-free flour of your choice. This will result in a slightly less stretchy cheez.

Gooey Grilled Cheez

These long-time sandwich favorites have all the goo and glory we love, but now they are low-fat and dairy free! If you like, serve them with a dab of grainy mustard spread on top.

See photo, facing p. 97

⅔ cup water

¼ cup nutritional yeast flakes

2 tablespoons flour (any kind; your choice)

1 tablespoons fresh lemon juice *(taste ADD ½ more if needed)*

2 tablespoons sesame tahini

1½ tablespoons ketchup

2 teaspoons kuzu, arrowroot, or cornstarch

1 teaspoon onion powder

¼ teaspoon each: garlic powder, turmeric, dry mustard, and salt

8 slices whole-grain or gluten-free rice bread

Combine all ingredients, except bread, in a medium saucepan, and whisk until mixture is smooth. Bring to a boil, stirring constantly with the wire whisk. Reduce heat to low and cook, stirring constantly, until mixture is very thick and smooth. Remove from heat. Place 4 of the bread slices on a flat surface. Cover one side of each slice evenly with the cooked mixture. Top with remaining bread slices.

Grill in a large, heavy skillet misted with nonstick cooking spray or coated with a small amount of vegetable oil or nonhydrogenated vegan margarine. Brown each side well, carefully turning over once. Slice sandwiches in half diagonally, and serve at once.

Pickled Grilled Cheez

Stir 1 tablespoon drained pickle relish (or more, to taste) into the cooked cheez mixture prior to spreading it on the bread.

FREE OF:
GLUTEN
SOY
NUTS
CORN

Per serving:	
calories	211
protein	10 g
fat	8 g
carbohydrate	29 g
calcium	79 mg
sodium	418 mg

Contains sesame tahini.

This low-fat snack is incredibly delicious. Serve it at parties or when watching your favorite movies.

Per serving:	
calories	30
protein	3 g
fat	0 g
carbohydrate	5 g
calcium	3 mg
sodium	135 mg

FREE OF:
GLUTEN
SOY
NUTS

Here's a cheezy corn chip snack that's perfect for parties. Be sure to use only fried tortilla chips, as the coating mix will not stick to baked chips.

Per serving:	
calories	154
protein	5 g
fat	6 g
carbohydrate	21 g
calcium	23 mg
sodium	66 mg

FREE OF:
GLUTEN
SOY
NUTS

Cheezy Popcorn

4 cups air-popped popcorn

Olive oil spray

⅓ cup nutritional yeast flakes

½ to 1 teaspoon chili powder or curry powder

½ teaspoon salt, or to taste

½ teaspoon garlic powder

¼ teaspoon onion powder

Place warm popcorn in a large bowl and mist it with olive oil. Toss gently and mist again. Repeat until all kernels are lightly coated with oil. Combine remaining ingredients in a zippered plastic bag. Seal bag and shake until well mixed. Drop in popcorn, a small quantity at a time, seal bag, and shake and turn bag to coat. Continue to add a small amount of popcorn to the bag until all kernels are well coated. Store in the zippered bag. Shake again gently just before serving.

Durritas

⅓ cup nutritional yeast flakes

½ to 1 teaspoon chili powder or curry powder

½ to 1 teaspoon garlic powder

½ teaspoon salt, or to taste

¼ to ½ teaspoon onion powder

8 ounces fried corn tortilla chips

Combine nutritional yeast flakes and seasonings in a zippered plastic bag. Shake until well mixed. Drop in corn chips, a small quantity at a time, seal bag, and shake and turn bag to coat, taking care not to break the chips. Continue to add a small amount of chips to the bag until all are well coated. Store in the zippered bag. Shake again gently just before serving.

SALADS AND DRESSINGS

I n this section you'll find a tantalizing assortment of mouth-watering salads that are perfect for lunch, brunch, or picnics. As a side dish, they beautifully complement sandwiches and soups. Many of the salads presented here can be served side by side to create a complete and satisfying meal, and some are hearty enough to go solo as the main attraction. For pasta salads, gluten-sensitive people should always use a gluten-free pasta (such as rice, quinoa, or corn pasta).

We also provide an array of tempting dressings that are well suited to top grains, pasta, potatoes, and vegetables, as well as standard salads of every variety. Rich, creamy, dairy-free dressings like these are much fresher and more delicious than anything found in a bottle, and they are so quick and easy to prepare that there's no excuse for your dressings to be anything but homemade.

This delectable mix of salad greens and vegetables is combined with faux feta cheese and an authentic Greek dressing. It makes a light, refreshing, warm weather meal. Serve it with pita bread and steamed rice on the side.

Greek Salad

Salad Mix

7 to 8 cups torn romaine lettuce

1 cup cherry tomatoes, cut in half

1 medium cucumber, peeled, halved, seeded, and sliced

2 medium carrots, shredded

1 green bell pepper, cut into 1-inch squares

½ cup sliced red onions

½ cup kalamata olives

½ cup drained, coarsely crumbled Betta Feta, page 45

Greek Dressing

½ cup extra-virgin olive oil

¼ cup red wine vinegar

1 teaspoon dried oregano

½ teaspoon sugar

Salt and pepper

Place torn romaine in a large salad bowl. Arrange tomatoes, cucumber, carrots, bell pepper, and red onion slices over it. Sprinkle olives and crumbled Betta Feta on top. If not planning to serve soon, cover with a damp paper towel and refrigerate for up to two hours. For dressing, whisk together olive oil, vinegar, oregano, sugar, and salt and pepper to taste. Just before serving, drizzle dressing over vegetables and toss gently.

Per 2 tablespoons:	
calories	199
protein	5 g
fat	17 g
carbohydrate	10 g
calcium	87 mg
sodium	315 mg

FREE OF:
GLUTEN
NUTS
YEAST
CORN

Contains vinegar.

Olive Cheez, page 162
Pepper Jack Cheez, page 165

Golden Pasta and Cauliflower Salad

MAKES 8 SERVINGS

Well dressed and delectable, this elegant salad is equally at home served warm or chilled. It makes a hearty, cool weather main dish as well as a welcome addition to hot weather picnics and year-round potluck suppers.

1 large head cauliflower, broken into bite-size florets

1 pound radiatore or corkscrew pasta

1 cup thinly sliced scallions

½ cup natural peanut, almond, or cashew butter

⅓ cup nutritional yeast flakes

¼ cup balsamic vinegar

¼ cup fresh lemon juice

1 tablespoon dark sesame oil

1¼ cups water

Several drops Tabasco

1 large red bell pepper, finely diced

1 (8 ounce) can sliced water chestnuts, drained

Cook pasta according to package directions. About 5 to 10 minutes before pasta is done (depending on the size of the florets and how crunchy or tender you like your cauliflower), add cauliflower and stir. Cook cauliflower and pasta together until pasta is tender. Drain well, rinse under cold water to stop the cooking, and drain again. Transfer to a large bowl. Stir in scallions and set aside.

Cream together nut butter, nutritional yeast flakes, vinegar, lemon juice, and sesame oil. Gradually add water, beating in a small amount at a time. When smooth, add Tabasco to taste. Pour over pasta and cauliflower, add bell pepper and water chestnuts, and toss gently but thoroughly until evenly distributed. Serve warm, chilled, or at room temperature.

FREE OF: GLUTEN SOY CORN

Per serving:	
calories	240
protein	12 g
fat	10 g
carbohydrate	30 g
calcium	38 mg
sodium	63 mg

Gazebo Cheezcake, page 168
Chocolate Almond Cheezcake, page 170

This vegan Caesar Salad captures the flavor of its namesake, even though it contains no eggs, dairy products, or anchovies. It's remarkably simple to make using basic pantry staples and the taste is out of this world.

Caesar Salad

Croutons

1½ cups French bread, sourdough bread, or whole-grain bread cubes

Caesar Dressing

3 tablespoons nutritional yeast flakes

2 tablespoons tahini

2 tablespoons Dijon mustard

½ teaspoon crushed garlic

⅓ cup water

3 tablespoons fresh lemon juice

1 tablespoon balsamic vinegar

Salad Mix

6 to 8 cups torn romaine lettuce

Optional Garnishes

Cracked black pepper (freshly ground, if possible)

Toasted nori flakes (see Tip next page)

Parmezano Sprinkles, page 50, or soy-based vegan parmesan alternative

Fresh lemon wedges

Preheat oven to 350°F. Spread bread cubes in a single layer in a large baking pan and bake until crisp and golden brown, about 15 minutes, stirring once or twice. (The croutons will not reach their full crispness until they have cooled.) Set aside.

To make the dressing, combine nutritional yeast flakes, tahini, mustard, and garlic in a medium bowl and stir together to make a paste. Gradually beat in the water, lemon juice, and vinegar, stirring vigorously with a wire whisk until very smooth and creamy.

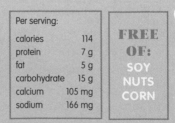

Per serving:

calories	114
protein	7 g
fat	5 g
carbohydrate	15 g
calcium	105 mg
sodium	166 mg

FREE OF:
SOY
NUTS
CORN

Contains sesame tahini.

146

To assemble the salad, place the lettuce in a large bowl. (The larger the better to facilitate tossing.) Pour dressing on top and toss until all pieces are well coated. Add croutons and toss again, making sure everything is well distributed. Divide equally among four salad plates or bowls. Garnish with cracked black pepper, toasted nori flakes, Parmezano Sprinkles, and lemon wedges, if desired. Serve immediately.

Tip: Nori is a sweet and delicate tasting sea vegetable that makes a great stand-in for the anchovy flavor traditionally associated with Caesar Salad. Its color is a lustrous, rich purple-black. Carefully toast nori over a gas flame or in a dry skillet until it turns bright green. Toasting nori makes it sweeter. Then crumble it into flakes. Alternatively, look for pretoasted "sushi nori" sheets, which you can crumble by hand or pulse into flakes in a food processor, or AO nori flakes (AO means green).

Pasta, vegetables, uncheese, and croutons mingle in a tantalizing pine nut dressing. This robust salad will tame even the most unruly appetites.

Chef's Salad with Pine Nut Vinaigrette

½ cup pine nuts

½ cup extra-virgin olive oil

½ cup water

¼ cup fresh lemon juice

¼ cup umeboshi plum vinegar

¼ cup balsamic vinegar

1 teaspoon dried oregano

½ teaspoon crushed garlic

¼ teaspoon pepper

1 pound radiatore or corkscrew pasta

1 large head Romaine lettuce, torn into bite-size pieces

3 fresh tomatoes, seeded and chopped

1 small red onion, thinly sliced into rings

½ cup Parmezano Sprinkles, page 50, or soy-based
   vegan parmesan alternative

1 block uncheese (your choice from pages 157 to 166), diced

3 cups croutons (optional)

To make the vinaigrette, toast nuts in a dry skillet over medium heat, stirring almost constantly, until golden, about 3 to 5 minutes. Remove from pan and place in a blender along with the oil, water, lemon juice, vinegars, oregano, garlic, and pepper. Process several minutes until completely smooth and creamy.

Cook pasta according to package directions. Rinse under cold water to cool. Drain well. Place in a very large bowl along with the lettuce, tomatoes, and onion. If not planning to serve soon, cover with a damp paper towel and refrigerate for up to two hours. Just before serving, pour dressing over all and toss gently. Sprinkle on Parmezano and toss again. Add cubed uncheese and croutons, if using, and toss gently but thoroughly one final time.

Per serving:	
calories	309
protein	10 g
fat	22 g
carbohydrate	24 g
calcium	82 mg
sodium	122 mg

FREE OF:
GLUTEN
SOY
CORN

Mediterranean Quinoa Salad

MAKES ABOUT 5 CUPS
(6 SERVINGS)

This hearty salad makes a great impression when served at a vegan barbecue or share-a-dish gathering. It tastes even better the following day.

1½ cups quinoa, rinsed well and drained

2¼ cups vegetable broth or water

2 large tomatoes, chopped

1 cup drained and coarsely crumbled Betta Feta, page 45

½ cup chopped fresh cilantro

½ cup sliced scallions

½ cup extra-virgin olive oil

½ cup fresh lemon juice

½ cup lightly toasted pine nuts

Salt and pepper

Bring broth or water to a boil. Add quinoa, reduce heat to low, and cover and cook for 15 minutes. Remove from heat and let rest for 5 minutes. Fluff with a fork and cool to room temperature. Fold tomatoes, Betta Feta, cilantro, and scallions into the quinoa. In a small bowl, whisk together oil, lemon juice, salt, and pepper. Pour over quinoa mixture and mix well. Gently stir in toasted pine nuts. Serve at once or chill thoroughly.

FREE OF:
GLUTEN
YEAST
CORN

Per serving:	
calories	430
protein	14 g
fat	32 g
carbohydrate	30 g
calcium	118 mg
sodium	251 mg

MAKES ABOUT 2¼ CUPS

At last, a vegan mayonnaise that is moderately low in fat, healthful, delicious, and soy-free! Use this creamy spread anywhere you would use mayonnaise—on sandwiches, in potato and pasta salads, or as a starting point for other sauces and dressings. You'll find endless ways to enjoy it, and every time you do you'll add a touch of luscious flavor and healthful dietary fiber, too!

Beannaise

2 cups drained cooked or canned white beans
   (one 15- or 16-ounce can)

2 tablespoons fresh lemon juice

1 tablespoon white wine vinegar

½ teaspoon salt

¼ teaspoon dry mustard

⅓ cup extra-virgin olive oil

⅓ cup organic canola or safflower oil (or a blend of both)

Place the beans, lemon juice, vinegar, salt, and dry mustard in a blender (for the smoothest dressing) or food processor fitted with a metal blade. Process until very creamy. With the appliance running, drizzle in the oils in a slow, steady stream through the cap opening in the lid. Continue processing until well blended, stopping to scrape down the sides of the container as needed. Chill thoroughly before using. Keeps about 7 days in the refrigerator. May be frozen.

Per 2 tablespoons:	
calories	96
protein	2 g
fat	8 g
carbohydrate	5 g
calcium	18 mg
sodium	60 mg

FREE OF:
GLUTEN
SOY
NUTS
YEAST
CORN

Contains vinegar. For a vinegar-free version, replace the vinegar with an addition tablespoon of lemon juice.

Deli Dressing

1½ cups (about 12 ounces) crumbled firm silken tofu

3 tablespoons fresh lemon juice

½ teaspoon salt

¼ teaspoon dry mustard

¼ cup extra-virgin olive or organic canola or safflower oil

Combine tofu, lemon juice, salt, and dry mustard in a blender or food processor and process until smooth and creamy. With appliance running, drizzle in oil in a slow steady stream through cap opening in the lid. Will keep for about 7 days in the refrigerator.

MAKES ABOUT 1½ CUPS

This is the perfect low-fat substitute for traditional egg-laden mayonnaise.

FREE OF: GLUTEN NUTS YEAST CORN	Per 2 tablespoons:	
	calories	63
	protein	3 g
	fat	6 g
	carbohydrate	1 g
	calcium	11 mg
	sodium	101 mg

Sour Dressing

1½ cups (about 12 ounces) crumbled firm silken tofu

2 tablespoons fresh lemon juice

1 tablespoon white wine vinegar

½ teaspoon salt

⅛ teaspoon ground coriander

2 tablespoons organic canola oil or extra-virgin olive oil

Place the tofu, lemon juice, vinegar, salt, and coriander in a blender (for the smoothest dressing) or food processor fitted with a metal blade. Process until very creamy. With the appliance running, drizzle in the oil in a slow, steady stream through the cap opening in the lid. Continue processing until well blended, stopping to scrape down the sides of the container as needed. Chill thoroughly before using. Keeps about 7 days in the refrigerator.

MAKES ABOUT 1½ CUPS

Use this sumptuous, creamy topping wherever you would use dairy sour cream.

FREE OF: GLUTEN NUTS YEAST CORN	Per 2 tablespoons:	
	calories	44
	protein	3 g
	fat	3 g
	carbohydrate	1 g
	calcium	11 mg
	sodium	101 mg

Contains vinegar. For a vinegar-free version, replace the vinegar with an addition tablespoon of lemon juice.

Everyone appreciates a great signature recipe that is unique yet universally beloved. Here is yours! It's simple and quick to make and perks up everything from salads and steamed veggies to rice, pasta, and potatoes. This "house dressing" stores well, so you can use it throughout the week, not just on special occasions. It's rich, but a little goes a long way!

Best-of-the-House Dressing

½ cup sesame tahini

¼ cup extra-virgin olive oil

1½ teaspoons dried mint

1¼ teaspoons salt

1 teaspoon garlic powder

1¼ cups water

½ cup fresh lemon juice

In a food processor, blender, or medium bowl, blend or whisk the tahini, olive oil, mint, salt, and garlic powder until creamy and smooth. Blend or whisk in the water in a slow, gradual stream. When smooth, blend or vigorously beat in the lemon juice until well combined. Keeps about 10 to 14 days in the refrigerator. Stir well before serving.

Variation: For a richer version, increase olive oil to ½ cup and reduce water to 1 cup.

Peppery House Dressing: Replace mint with 1½ tea-spoons finely ground black pepper and ¼ teaspoon finely crumbled dried oregano (optional).

Per 2 tablespoons:	
calories	60
protein	1 g
fat	6 g
carbohydrate	2 g
calcium	26 mg
sodium	138 mg

FREE OF:
GLUTEN
SOY
NUTS
YEAST
CORN

Contains sesame tahini.

Creamy Bleu Cheez Dressing

½ cup sesame tahini

½ cup extra-virgin olive oil

1¼ teaspoons salt

1 teaspoon crushed garlic or garlic powder

1 teaspoon light or chickpea miso

¼ teaspoon white pepper

1 cup water

¼ cup fresh lemon juice

¼ cup white wine vinegar

1 teaspoon dried parsley flakes, or 1 tablespoon
   minced fresh parsley

In a medium bowl, beat together tahini, olive oil, salt, garlic or garlic powder, miso, and pepper until creamy and smooth. Whisk in water in a slow, gradual stream. When smooth, vigor–ously beat in lemon juice and vinegar until well combined. Stir in parsley. Keeps about 10 to 14 days in the refrigerator. Stir well before serving.

MAKES ABOUT 2½ CUPS

Nothing inspires compliments like a rich, cheesy salad dressing with an exquisite "aged" flavor. Here is a dairy-free bleu cheez dressing made with pure, natural ingredients, replete with timeless appeal.

FREE OF:
GLUTEN
SOY
NUTS
YEAST
CORN

Per 2 tablespoons:	
calories	84
protein	1 g
fat	8 g
carbohydrate	2 g
calcium	26 mg
sodium	144 mg

Contains sesame tahini.
Contains vinegar and miso.

MAKES ABOUT 2½ CUPS

This creamy dressing is a beautiful pale green with a dazzling taste to match. It's great on salads, of course, but try it as a sauce for vegetables, grains, and potatoes, too. It also makes a delicious dip.

Green Goddess Dressing

1½ cups plain nondairy milk or water

2 tablespoons umeboshi plum paste

⅓ cup sesame tahini

⅓ cup minced fresh parsley

2 tablespoons extra-virgin olive oil

1 large scallion, sliced

1½ teaspoons dried tarragon

½ teaspoon crushed garlic or garlic powder

Pinch of white pepper

Salt

Combine all the ingredients in a blender and process several minutes until creamy and completely smooth (make sure no green flecks of parsley or scallion remain). Keeps about 7 days in the refrigerator. Stir well before serving.

Per 2 tablespoons:	
calories	43
protein	1 g
fat	4 g
carbohydrate	2 g
calcium	18 mg
sodium	47 mg

FREE OF:
GLUTEN
SOY
NUTS
YEAST
CORN

Contains sesame tahini.
Contains umeboshi plum paste.

"Sea" Sar Dressing

MAKES ABOUT 2⅓ CUPS

1½ cups (about 12 ounces) crumbled firm silken tofu, or 2 cups
  drained cooked or canned white beans (one 15- or 16-ounce can)

10 pitted large green olives

3 to 6 tablespoons water (use smaller amount if using tofu;
  use larger amount if using beans)

2 tablespoons green nori flakes

2 tablespoons fresh lemon juice

1 tablespoon olive brine or white wine vinegar

1 tablespoon nutritional yeast flakes

1 tablespoon Dijon mustard

1 teaspoon crushed garlic

1 teaspoon black pepper

½ teaspoon salt

½ cup extra-virgin olive oil

Combine all the ingredients, except olive oil, in a blender and process several minutes until creamy and completely smooth. With blender running, slowly drizzle in the olive oil through the cap opening in the lid until thoroughly incorporated. Keeps about 7 days in the refrigerator. Stir well before serving.

This outstanding vegan version of the classic Caesar dressing was inspired by the gourmet, award-winning, vegetarian restaurant It's Only Natural (www.ionrestaurant.com) in Middletown, Connecticut, where owners Mark Shadle and Lisa Magee offer an unparalleled Caesar salad. The olives give the dressing bite, while the nori replaces the anchovies. It has a very rich flavor, so a little goes a long way. It's also a treat on potatoes or even grated cabbage and carrots for a very special coleslaw. If you like a robust spread for sandwiches, try this dressing instead of mayonnaise.

FREE OF:
GLUTEN
SOY
NUTS
CORN

Per 2 tablespoons:	
calories	69
protein	2 g
fat	7 g
carbohydrate	1 g
calcium	8 mg
sodium	113 mg

MAKES 2 CUPS

Everyone loves a rich, chunky, flavorful dressing. This one is delightful as a dip with raw or steamed veggies or as a topping for crunchy fresh salads, especially ones with beans. Also try it with chopped raw or cooked vegetables over split baked potatoes.

Chunky Roquefort Dip and Dressing

¼ pound (4 ounces) firm regular tofu, drained

1½ cups (about 12 ounces) crumbled firm silken tofu

½ cup plain nondairy milk

1 tablespoon sesame tahini

4 teaspoons umeboshi plum paste

1 teaspoon nutritional yeast flakes

½ to 1 teaspoon crushed garlic

Pinch of white pepper

1 tablespoon minced fresh parsley, or 1½ teaspoons dried parsley

Break tofu into large chunks. Place in a saucepan and cover with water. Bring to a boil, reduce heat, and simmer 5 minutes. Drain well. Chill uncovered in the refrigerator until cool enough to handle. Crumble and set aside. Place remaining ingredients, except parsley, in a food processor and process until very smooth and creamy. Mixture will be very thick. Briefly pulse in parsley and reserved tofu, keeping the tofu in small to mid–size chunks. Chill several hours or overnight before serving to allow flavors to blend. Keeps 5 to 7 days in the refrigerator.

Per 2 tablespoons:	
calories	38
protein	4 g
fat	2 g
carbohydrate	2 g
calcium	28 mg
sodium	63 mg

FREE OF:
GLUTEN
NUTS
CORN

Contains sesame tahini.

BLOCK UNCHEESES

Block cheeses are among the most challenging to convert to dairy-free versions. This is largely because homemade uncheeses are comparatively low in fat—specifically saturated fat, which stays hard and solid at room temperature. Saturated fat is what keeps dairy cheeses firm, sliceable, and easy to grate. Consequently, uncheese blocks generally are much softer than their dairy counterparts and require a lighter touch and more gentle handling when being sliced or grated. One way around this is to freeze uncheese blocks and grate them when they are partially thawed. However, once fully thawed, the texture and consistency may be altered a bit, depending on the particular cheez. For this reason, it's a good idea to freeze only the amount you know you will be grating and using shortly.

Melting has been a challenge with uncheeses from the outset. This is why so many manufacturers add dairy-derived casein to their uncheese products—it improves meltability and achieves the "stretch" that is characteristic of dairy cheese. Fortunately, homemade, dairy-free uncheeses will melt, although you might want to give them a little nudge in the process. Covering uncheeses during cooking or baking keeps in heat and moisture and helps promote more even melting. To brown uncheeses after melting, uncover and place under the broiler. Misting with oil will also help to promote better browning and melting.

Important Notes: Unless a particular shape of container is specified in a recipe, any shape container (square, round, rectangular, or tube-shaped) will work with the block uncheeses as long as the sides are straight and do not slope inward. Inward sloping sides will make it impossible to remove the uncheese as a block.

• When simmering agar flakes or powder, be sure the agar is dissolved completely before adding the mixture to the blender. To soften the agar, which will help it dissolve, let it soak in the water for 5 to 10 minutes before bringing to a boil.

• For richer tasting block uncheeses, use soymilk instead of water and/or add a tablespoon or two of mild vegetable oil while blending.

Block uncheeses can be enjoyed in all the same ways you might previously have used dairy cheeses. Here are just a few ideas:

- cube and toss with salads
- thinly slice and layer in or on top of casseroles
- grate or cube and add to soups or baked dishes
- slice and layer on cold or grilled sandwiches
- cube and skewer with toothpicks for hors d'oeuvres
- grate and add to stuffed vegetables
- grate or cube and add to savory dinner pies
- grate and sprinkle over baked potatoes
- grate and sprinkle over pizza (this works best if the grated uncheese is tossed or misted with oil)
- thinly slice and melt on top of veggie burgers
- cube and stir into hot sauces and gravies
- thinly slice and serve on crackers
- cube or grate and toss with hot grains
- cube or grate and toss with hot steamed vegetables

Swizz Cheez

Enjoy this versatile, tangy, white cheez. It's ideal for gentle shredding, melting, toasting in sandwiches, and, of course, snacking.

1½ cups water

5 tablespoons agar flakes, or 1½ tablespoons agar powder

½ cup chopped raw cashews or skinless Brazil nuts

¼ cup nutritional yeast flakes

3 tablespoons fresh lemon juice

2 tablespoons sesame tahini

1 tablespoon onion powder

2 teaspoons Dijon mustard

½ teaspoon garlic powder

½ teaspoon dry mustard

¼ teaspoon ground dill seed or ground coriander

¼ teaspoon salt, or to taste

Lightly oil a 3-cup plastic storage container and set aside. Combine the water and agar in a small saucepan and bring to a boil. Reduce the heat and simmer, stirring often, until dissolved, about 5 to 10 minutes. Transfer to a blender and add the remaining ingredients. Process several minutes until completely smooth, scraping down the sides of the blender jar as necessary. Pour into the prepared container and cool uncovered in the refrigerator. When completely cool, cover and chill several hours or overnight. To serve, turn out of the container and slice. Store leftovers covered in the refrigerator. Will keep 5 to 7 days.

FREE OF:
GLUTEN
SOY
CORN

Per 2 tablespoons:	
calories	38
protein	2 g
fat	3 g
carbohydrate	3 g
calcium	14 mg
sodium	36 mg

This piquant uncheese is fragrant and delectable and easily slices into thick slabs or paper-thin shavings.

Onion, Dill, and Horseradish Cheez

1½ cups water

5 tablespoons agar flakes, or 1½ tablespoons agar powder

½ cup chopped raw cashews

¼ cup nutritional yeast flakes

3 tablespoons fresh lemon juice

2 tablespoons tahini

2 tablespoons white horseradish (not creamed)

2 teaspoons Dijon mustard

1 teaspoon salt

1 teaspoon onion powder

¼ teaspoon garlic powder

3 tablespoons dried onion flakes

2 teaspoons dried dillweed

Lightly oil a 3-cup plastic storage container and set aside. Combine the water and agar in a small saucepan and bring to a boil. Reduce the heat and simmer, stirring often, for 5 to 10 minutes, or until completely dissolved. Transfer to a blender and add the cashews, nutritional yeast, tahini, horseradish, mustard, salt, onion powder, and garlic powder. Process several minutes until completely smooth, scraping down the sides of the blender jar as necessary. By hand, stir in the onion flakes and dillweed. Pour into the prepared container and cool uncovered in the refrigerator. When completely cool, cover and chill several hours or overnight. To serve, turn out of the container and slice. Store leftovers covered in the refrigerator. Will keep 5 to 7 days..

Per 2 tablespoons:

calories	32
protein	1 g
fat	2 g
carbohydrate	2 g
calcium	12 mg
sodium	97 mg

FREE OF:
GLUTEN
SOY
CORN

Gooda Cheez

1¾ cups water

½ cup chopped carrots

5 tablespoons agar flakes, or 1½ tablespoons agar powder

½ cup chopped raw cashews

¼ cup nutritional yeast flakes

3 tablespoons sesame tahini

3 tablespoons fresh lemon juice

1 tablespoon Dijon mustard

2 teaspoons onion powder

1 teaspoon salt

½ teaspoon garlic powder

½ teaspoon dry mustard

¼ teaspoon turmeric

¼ teaspoon paprika

¼ teaspoon ground cumin

This impressive, dome-shaped cheez has a creamy texture and lovely golden color. Slice it into wedges for a delectable snack or appetizer. For Smoked Gooda, add a few drops of liquid hickory smoke or a pinch of hickory salt while blending. Store leftovers covered in the refrigerator; keeps 5 to 7 days.

Lightly oil a 3-cup bowl or mold with a rounded bottom and set aside. Combine the water and carrots in a saucepan and bring to a boil. Reduce heat, cover, and cook until very tender, about 10 to 15 minutes. Remove lid and stir in agar flakes. Bring to a boil again. Reduce heat and simmer, stirring often, until agar is dissolved, about 5 to 10 minutes longer.

Transfer to a blender and add the remaining ingredients. Process several minutes until completely smooth, scraping down the sides of the blender jar as necessary. Pour into the prepared container and smooth the top. Cool uncovered in the refrigerator. When completely cool, cover and chill several hours or overnight. To serve, turn out of the mold and slice into wedges.

FREE OF:
GLUTEN
SOY
CORN

Per 2 tablespoons:	
calories	37
protein	2 g
fat	2 g
carbohydrate	3 g
calcium	15 mg
sodium	100 mg

This is a tangy but mild, orange-colored cheez that slices well for sandwiches and snacks. It also makes fantastic grilled cheez sandwiches. If you like, shred it with a light touch and sprinkle it over salads or baked potatoes.

See photo (Olive Cheez), facing p. 144

Colby Cheez

1½ cups water

5 tablespoons agar flakes, or 1½ tablespoons agar powder

½ cup roasted red peppers (skin and seeds removed), or pimiento pieces

½ cup chopped raw cashews or skinless Brazil nuts

¼ cup nutritional yeast flakes

3 tablespoons fresh lemon juice

2 tablespoons sesame tahini

2 teaspoons onion powder

1 teaspoon salt

¼ teaspoon garlic powder

¼ teaspoon dry mustard

Lightly oil a 3–cup plastic storage container and set aside. Combine the water and agar in a small saucepan and bring to a boil. Reduce the heat and simmer, stirring often, until dissolved, about 5 to 10 minutes. Transfer to a blender and add the remaining ingredients. Process several minutes until completely smooth, scraping down the sides of the blender jar as necessary. Pour into the prepared container and cool uncovered in the refrigerator. When completely cool, cover and chill several hours or overnight. To serve, turn out of the container and slice. Store leftovers covered in the refrigerator. Will keep 5 to 7 days.

Variations: In place of the red peppers, use ½ cup cooked chopped carrots, 2 to 3 teaspoons paprika, or 2 tablespoons unsalted tomato paste.

Chedda Cheez: Add 2 tablespoons light or chickpea miso prior to blending.

Olive Cheez: Replace dry mustard with 1 tablespoon Dijon mustard. After blending, stir in ¾ cup chopped black olives or sliced pimiento–stuffed green olives.

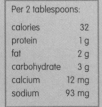

Per 2 tablespoons:	
calories	32
protein	1 g
fat	2 g
carbohydrate	3 g
calcium	12 mg
sodium	93 mg

FREE OF:
GLUTEN
SOY
CORN

Buffalo Mostarella

2 cups water or plain soymilk

½ cup nutritional yeast flakes

1/3 cup quick-cooking rolled oats

¼ cup sesame tahini

¼ cup kuzu, arrowroot, or cornstarch

3 to 4 tablespoons fresh lemon juice

1 tablespoon onion powder

1 teaspoon salt

Lightly oil a 3-cup rectangular mold, loaf pan, or other small rectangular or oval container. Alternatively, for round slices, oil a small, straight-sided, cylindrical container.

Combine all ingredients in a blender and process several minutes until completely smooth. Pour into a saucepan and cook and stir over medium heat until very thick and smooth. Pack into the prepared container. Cool uncovered in the refrigerator. When completely cool, cover and chill overnight. To serve, turn out of the mold and carefully slice with an oiled or water-moistened knife (the cheez will be very soft and a bit sticky). Store leftovers covered in the refrigerator. Will keep about 5 to 7 days.

Smoky Fresh Provolone

Prepare recipe as directed, but during cooking add a pinch of hickory salt or several drops of liquid hickory smoke to taste.

MAKES 3 CUPS

At last—wonderful, fresh "mozzarella" cheez! Buffalo Mostarella, like its fresh dairy counterpart, is moist and soft, quick melting, and delicate tasting—there is no comparison to the rubbery, commercialized dairy product available in supermarkets. It has a very mild, creamy, faintly sour flavor and, because it melts so beautifully and quickly, it's extremely good used in sauces, pasta dishes, and, of course, as a pizza topping. It's also perfect for creating a magnificent Italian-style salad of ripe tomatoes, fresh basil, and Buffalo Mostarella.

FREE OF: SOY NUTS CORN

Per 2 tablespoons:	
calories	32
protein	2 g
fat	1 g
carbohydrate	4 g
calcium	13 mg
sodium	92 mg

This mild uncheese complements almost every food. Serve it in slices with crisp fruits such as pears or apples, add diced cubes to your favorite steamed vegetables, or create cold sandwiches or toasty grilled cheez.

Muenster Cheez

Paprika

1½ cups water

5 tablespoons agar flakes, or 1½ tablespoons agar powder

½ cup firm silken tofu (optional)

½ cup chopped raw cashews or skinless Brazil nuts

¼ cup nutritional yeast flakes

¼ cup fresh lemon juice

2 tablespoons sesame tahini

2 teaspoons onion powder

1 teaspoon salt

½ teaspoon dry mustard

¼ teaspoon garlic powder

¼ teaspoon ground caraway seeds or coriander

Lightly oil a 3-cup plastic storage container, and sprinkle paprika over the sides and bottom until lightly coated. Set aside. Combine the water and agar in a small saucepan and bring to a boil. Reduce the heat and simmer, stirring often, until dissolved, about 5 to 10 minutes. Transfer to a blender and add the remaining ingredients. Process several minutes until completely smooth, scraping down the sides of the blender jar as necessary. Pour into the prepared container and cool uncovered in the refrigerator. When completely cool, cover and chill several hours or overnight. To serve, turn out of the container and slice. Store leftovers covered in the refrigerator. Will keep 5 to 7 days.

Per 2 tablespoons:

calories	32
protein	1 g
fat	2 g
carbohydrate	2 g
calcium	12 mg
sodium	93 mg

FREE OF:
GLUTEN
SOY
CORN

Monterey Jack Cheez

1½ cups water

5 tablespoons agar flakes, or 1½ tablespoons agar powder

½ cup firm silken tofu (optional)

½ cup chopped raw cashews or skinless Brazil nuts

¼ cup nutritional yeast flakes

¼ cup fresh lemon juice

2 tablespoons sesame tahini

2 teaspoons onion powder

1 teaspoon salt

½ teaspoon dry mustard

¼ teaspoon garlic powder

¼ teaspoon ground caraway seeds or coriander

This mild, white cheez is delicate in flavor, which makes it highly adaptable. Enjoy it "plain" or experiment with adding garlic, your favorite dried herbs and spices, peppery hot chilies, or chopped or sliced green and ripe olives.

See photo (Pepper Jack Cheez), facing p. 144

Lightly oil a 3-cup plastic storage container, and set aside. Combine the water and agar in a small saucepan and bring to a boil. Reduce the heat and simmer, stirring often, until dissolved, about 5 to 10 minutes. Transfer to a blender and add the remaining ingredients. Process several minutes until completely smooth, scraping down the sides of the blender jar as necessary. Pour into the prepared container and cool uncovered in the refrigerator. When completely cool, cover and chill several hours or overnight. To serve, turn out of the container and slice. Store leftovers covered in the refrigerator. Will keep 5 to 7 days.

Pepper Jack Cheez: Prepare Monterey Jack Cheez above. Stir crushed, dried red chili peppers and minced hot green chiles (or crushed black pepper) to taste into the blended mixture.

Caraway Jack Cheez: Prepare basic Monterey Jack Cheez as directed but increase caraway seeds to 1 tablespoon. Whole seeds may be used, if preferred.

FREE OF: GLUTEN SOY CORN	Per 2 tablespoons:	
	calories	32
	protein	1 g
	fat	2 g
	carbohydrate	2 g
	calcium	12 mg
	sodium	93 mg

**MAKES 1 WHEEL
(ABOUT 2½ CUPS)**

This lovely round of creamy cheez is delectable by itself. It's also delicious on crackers or sandwiches and is especially elegant as a snack or dessert served with fresh, crisp fruit, such as Asian pears. This versatile uncheese also makes a terrific pizza topping. Slice it thinly or thickly into wedges.

Brie

1 to 2 tablespoons wheat germ, or ⅓ cup toasted sliced almonds

1½ cups water

3 tablespoons agar flakes, or 1 tablespoon agar powder

½ cup chopped raw cashews

½ cup crumbled firm silken tofu

¼ cup nutritional yeast flakes

¼ cup fresh lemon juice

2 tablespoons sesame tahini

1½ teaspoons onion powder

1 teaspoon salt

¼ teaspoon garlic powder

⅛ teaspoon ground dill seed or ground coriander

Lightly oil a 2½-cup round, shallow mold, pie plate, or single layer round cake pan and dust it with the wheat germ or sprinkle the bottom with the toasted sliced almonds, spreading them as evenly as possible. Set aside. Combine the water and agar in a small saucepan and bring to a boil. Reduce the heat and simmer, stirring often, until dissolved, about 5 to 10 minutes.

Transfer to a blender and add the remaining ingredients. Process several minutes until completely smooth, scraping down the sides of the blender jar as necessary. Pour into the prepared container. Cool uncovered in the refrigerator. When completely cool, cover and chill several hours or overnight. To serve, turn out by inverting the mold onto a large round plate (the wheat germ or almond-coated side will now be on top) and slice into wedges. Store leftovers covered in refrigerator. Will keep 5 to 7 days.

Per 2 tablespoons:	
calories	44
protein	2 g
fat	3 g
carbohydrate	3 g
calcium	15 mg
sodium	113 mg

**FREE OF:
GLUTEN
CORN**

SWEETS

We tend to think of desserts as sweet and cheese as savory and therefore an unlikely match. Nevertheless, cheese has found its way into a number of popular desserts, most conspicuously cheesecakes and pastries made with rich, sweetened cream cheese and other high-fat dairy products. Ordinarily, these foods would be off-limits for people watching their waistline, cholesterol, and fat intake. Fortunately, there's an effortless way to have your cheesecake and eat it, too—simply by making an uncheesecake!

The recipes in this section are deceptively healthful and decadently delicious. They will impress your family and wow your guests at holiday dinners and other celebrations. But don't save them for special occasions. Whenever you want to indulge your sweet tooth, spoil yourself with these scrumptious treats. They're fun to prepare and a pleasure to eat.

You'll also find a variety of crust recipes that are suitable for any dessert pie or uncheesecake. If you're in a rush, however, feel free to use a store-bought crust when necessary. Here are a few more cheezy dessert ideas for your enjoyment:

Chedda Topped Apple or Peach Pie: Prepare your favorite fresh or frozen apple or peach pie. Serve warm from the oven, and top each serving with a thin slice of Colby Cheez, page 162.

Fruit and Cheez: Serve fresh fruit or berries with slices of Muenster, page 164, Monterey Jack, page 165, Colby, page 162, or Swizz Cheez, page 159. Wedges of Brie or Gooda, pages 166 and 161, are particularly elegant as dessert cheezes.

Fruitwiches: For a snack or unique dessert, smear crisp apple or pear wedges with a dab of Gee Whiz Spread, page 39. A tall glass of your favorite wine, champagne, or sparkling cider will make this simple treat truly special.

This is a deli-style cheezcake—dense and hefty. Top it with sliced strawberries, blueberries, or fresh peaches when in season.

See photo, facing p. 145

Gazebo Cheezcake

1 crust of your choice (see Tip below)

1¼ cups water

¾ cup raw cashews

⅔ cup pure maple syrup

½ cup brown rice syrup

¼ cup fresh lemon juice

¼ cup agar flakes, or 2½ teaspoons agar powder

3 tablespoons kuzu, arrowroot, or cornstarch

1 tablespoon vanilla extract

1 teaspoon salt

1 pound firm regular tofu, crumbled

Preheat oven to 350°F. Prepare crust in an oiled 8–, 9–, or 10–inch springform pan or 10–inch pie plate. Place all the ingredients, except tofu, in a blender and process several minutes until completely smooth. Pour half of mixture into a bowl and set aside. Gradually add half of the tofu to the remaining mixture in the blender and process until velvety smooth. Pour carefully and evenly over the prepared crust. Return reserved mixture to the blender and gradually add the remaining tofu, once again processing until completely smooth. Pour over the mixture already in the crust and smooth out the surface.

Bake 60 minutes. Cool at room temperature, then chill at least 4 hours before serving. The top may crack a bit while cooling; this is characteristic of cheesecakes. Remove the outer ring of the springform pan before slicing.

Tip: Choose from the following crusts: Graham Cracker or Granola Nut Crust, page 181, or Caramel Nut Crust, page 180.

Per slice:	
calories	250
protein	6 g
fat	11 g
carbohydrate	34 g
calcium	78 mg
sodium	251 mg

FREE OF:
YEAST
CORN

Lemon Teasecake

1 recipe Granola Nut Crust, page 181, fully baked (use an
   8- or 9-inch springform pan), or Raw Nut Crust, page 180

½ cup uncooked millet

2 cups water

½ cup raw cashews

⅓ cup fresh lemon juice

⅓ cup pure maple syrup

2 teaspoons vanilla extract

1 teaspoon lemon extract

For many years, visitors to Seattle enjoyed dining at Cafe Ambrosia. This recipe is an adaptation of one of the restaurant's scrumptious signature desserts, developed by executive chef Francis Janes.

Note: For Key Lime Teasecake, replace the lemon juice with an equal amount of key lime juice.

Fully bake pie crust as directed (unless using Raw Nut Crust) and cool completely. Set aside.

In a medium saucepan with tight fitting lid, bring millet and water to a boil. Cover and simmer over low heat until water is absorbed and millet is soft, about 50 minutes. While millet is cooking, place cashews, lemon juice, maple syrup, and extracts in a blender. Process several minutes until perfectly smooth. If necessary, scrape down sides of the blender jar with a spatula and process for another minute. While cooked millet is still warm, add to blender mixture. Process another 3 minutes until creamy. Pour into the cooled crust.

Cool pie 30 minutes at room temperature. Place in the refrigerator and chill at least 4 hours before serving. Place plastic wrap over surface to prevent excess cracking. Teasecake will keep in the refrigerator about 3 days.

Toppings (optional)

• 8 ounces cherry preserves (fruit juice sweetened jam)

• 2 kiwifruit, peeled and sliced thin into rounds

FREE OF:
GLUTEN SOY YEAST CORN

Per slice:	
calories	231
protein	4 g
fat	10 g
carbohydrate	33 g
calcium	21 mg
sodium	110 mg

For all those special occasions when you really want to astound your guests, remember that no one can resist chocolate cheezcake!

See photo, facing p. 145

Chocolate Almond Cheezcake

1 crust of your choice (see Tip below)

1½ cups water

1½ cups pure maple syrup

¾ cup raw cashews

½ cup unsweetened cocoa powder

¼ cup agar flakes, or 2½ teaspoons agar powder

3 tablespoons kuzu, arrowroot, or cornstarch

2 teaspoons almond extract

1 teaspoon salt

1 pound firm regular tofu, crumbled

Preheat oven to 350°F. Prepare crust in an oiled 8–, 9–, or 10–inch springform pan or 10–inch pie plate. Place all the ingredients, except tofu, in a blender and process several minutes until completely smooth. Pour half of the mixture into a bowl and set aside. Gradually add half of the tofu to the remaining mixture in the blender, and process until velvety smooth. Pour carefully and evenly over the prepared crust. Return reserved mixture to the blender, and gradually add the remaining tofu, once again processing until completely smooth. Pour over the mixture already in the crust, and smooth out the surface.

Bake 60 minutes. Cool at room temperature, then chill at least 4 hours before serving. The top may crack a bit while cooling; this is characteristic of cheesecakes. Remove the outer ring of the springform pan before slicing.

Tip: Choose from the following crusts: Graham Cracker or Granola Nut Crust, page 181, or Caramel Nut Crust, page 180.

Per slice:		FREE OF:
calories	246	NUTS
protein	5 g	YEAST
fat	11 g	CORN
carbohydrate	36 g	
calcium	64 mg	
sodium	250 mg	

Contains almond extract.

Pumpkin Cheezcake

This creamy, spiced cheezcake is homey and inviting for special holiday gatherings or a delightful surprise dessert any season of the year.

1 crust of your choice (see Tip below)

1⅓ cups water

1⅓ cups canned pumpkin

1 cup pure maple syrup

¼ cup agar flakes, or 2½ teaspoons agar powder

3 tablespoons kuzu, arrowroot, or cornstarch

2 tablespoons fresh lemon juice

2 teaspoons vanilla extract

2 teaspoons ground cinnamon

1 teaspoon salt

1 teaspoon ground ginger

¼ teaspoon ground cloves

1 pound firm regular tofu, crumbled

Preheat oven to 350°F. Prepare crust in an oiled 8-, 9-, or 10-inch springform pan or 10-inch pie plate. Place all the ingredients, except tofu, in a blender and process several minutes until completely smooth. Pour half of the mixture into a bowl and set aside. Gradually add half of the tofu to the remaining mixture in the blender and process until velvety smooth. Pour carefully and evenly over the prepared crust. Return the reserved mixture to the blender and gradually add the remaining tofu, once again processing until completely smooth. Pour over the mixture already in the crust and smooth out the surface.

Bake 60 minutes. Cool at room temperature, then chill at least 4 hours before serving. The top may crack a bit while cooling; this is characteristic of cheesecakes. Remove the outer ring of the springform pan before slicing.

Tip: Choose from the following crusts: Graham Cracker or Granola Nut Crust, page 181, or Caramel Nut Crust, page 180.

FREE OF:
NUTS
YEAST
CORN

Per slice:	
calories	150
protein	5 g
fat	8 g
carbohydrate	16 g
calcium	72 mg
sodium	249 mg

Here's an easy, no-bake cheez-pie to impress your friends and family and create warm memories.

Ricotta Cheezcake Pie

1 (10-inch) pie crust of your choice, pages 178 to 181

1 cup water

2½ tablespoons agar flakes, or 2 teaspoons agar powder

½ pound firm regular tofu, crumbled

1½ cups (about 12 ounces) crumbled firm silken tofu

⅔ cup pure maple syrup

3 tablespoons fresh lemon juice

2 teaspoons vanilla extract

¼ teaspoon salt

Fresh berries for garnish (optional)

Place the water and agar flakes in a small saucepan and bring to a boil stirring constantly. Reduce heat and simmer until completely dissolved, about 5 to 10 minutes, stirring often.

Meanwhile, combine the remaining ingredients, except fruit, in a blender and process about 2 minutes. Pour agar mixture into blender with tofu mixture and process several minutes until velvety smooth.

Pour into the prepared crust. Refrigerate until well chilled and set, about 6 to 8 hours or overnight. If desired, top each serving with fresh whole raspberries, blueberries, or sliced strawberries.

Chocolate Cheezcake Pie

Omit the lemon juice and substitute ⅓ cup unsweetened cocoa powder. Reduce vanilla extract to 1½ teaspoons.

Per slice:	
calories	330
protein	10 g
fat	15 g
carbohydrate	41 g
calcium	102 mg
sodium	312 mg

FREE OF:
GLUTEN
NUTS
YEAST
CORN

This recipe can be gluten free or nut free depending on the crust you select.

Peanut Butter Fudge Pie

At last—the dessert of choice for the chocolate lover in us all. It's rich, fudgy, and peanut-buttery!

1 (10-inch) pie crust of your choice, pages 178 to 181

1⅓ cups water

3 tablespoons agar flakes, or 2 teaspoons agar powder

¾ cup mashed firm silken tofu

1¼ cups pure maple syrup

½ cup peanut butter

½ cup unsweetened cocoa powder

2 teaspoons vanilla extract

¼ teaspoon salt

Fully bake pie crust as directed (unless using Raw Nut Crust, page 180) and cool completely. Set aside.

For filling, combine water and agar flakes in a small saucepan and bring to a boil stirring constantly. Reduce heat and simmer until completely dissolved, about 5 to 10 minutes, stirring often. Pour into a blender along with remaining ingredients. Process several minutes until completely smooth. Pour into prepared pie crust. Refrigerate several hours or overnight before serving (best served thoroughly chilled).

Almond Butter Fudge Pie

Replace peanut butter with almond butter.

FREE OF:
GLUTEN
NUTS
YEAST
CORN

Per slice:	
calories	352
protein	7 g
fat	16 g
carbohydrate	49 g
calcium	56 mg
sodium	272 mg

This recipe can be gluten free or nut free depending on the crust you select. Contains peanuts.

MAKES ABOUT **8** SERVINGS

This no-bake chiffon pie makes a glorious presentation.

Apricot Creme Pie

1 (10-inch) pie crust of your choice, pages 178 to 181

1¾ cups water

8 ounces dried apricot halves

2 tablespoons agar flakes, or 1½ teaspoons agar powder

2 cups mashed firm silken tofu

½ cup pure maple syrup

1½ teaspoons vanilla extract

9 apricot halves (reserved from above)

1 tablespoon brown rice syrup

1 tablespoon water

Few drops vanilla extract (optional)

Fully bake pie crust as directed (unless using Raw Nut Crust) and cool completely. Set aside.

For the filling, place water and apricot halves in a medium saucepan and bring to a boil. Boil 1 minute. Remove from heat and let cool to room temperature. When cool, drain and reserve the cooking water. Remove 9 of the most attractive apricot halves and set them aside for the topping.

Return the apricot cooking water to the pan and stir in the agar flakes or powder. Bring to a boil, reduce heat, and simmer, stirring often, until completely dissolved, about 5 to 10 minutes. Pour into a blender along with the cooled apricots, tofu, maple syrup, and vanilla extract, and process several minutes until completely smooth. Pour into the cooled pie crust.

For the topping, glaze the reserved apricot halves by combining them in a small saucepan with the brown rice syrup, water, and vanilla extract, if using. Cook until the liquid has evaporated and apricots have a nice sheen. Place one apricot half in the center of the pie and arrange the other eight apricots evenly around the outer edge. Refrigerate several hours or overnight before serving.

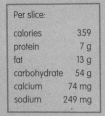

Per slice:	
calories	359
protein	7 g
fat	13 g
carbohydrate	54 g
calcium	74 mg
sodium	249 mg

FREE OF:
GLUTEN
NUTS
YEAST
CORN

This recipe can be gluten free or nut free depending on the crust you select.

Mocha Fudge Pie

1 (10-inch) pie crust of your choice, pages 178 to 181

¾ cups water

3 tablespoons agar flakes, or 2½ teaspoons agar powder

1 tablespoon instant coffee or powdered coffee substitute (not reconstituted)

2 cups mashed firm silken tofu

1 cup pure maple syrup

⅓ cup cashews, or 3 tablespoons cashew butter (optional, but highly recommended)

½ cup unsweetened cocoa powder

2 teaspoons vanilla extract

¼ teaspoon salt

Pinch of ground cinnamon (optional)

Decadently delicious! Fudge pies typically are made with chocolate squares containing hydrogenated fat, eggs, and high-fat dairy products such as butter and cream. This recipe proves that sweet, rich-tasting desserts can be dairy-free and wholesome, too!

Fully bake pie crust as directed (unless using Raw Nut Crust) and cool completely. Set aside.

For the filling, place water, agar, and instant coffee or coffee substitute granules in a small saucepan. Bring to a boil, reduce heat, and simmer, stirring often, until agar is completely dissolved, about 5 to 10 minutes. Pour into a blender along with the remaining ingredients and process several minutes until completely smooth. Pour into the cooled pie crust. Refrigerate several hours or overnight before serving (best if served thoroughly chilled). If you would like to add a special touch, top each slice with a dollop of Tofu Whipped Topping, page 177.

FREE OF:
GLUTEN
NUTS
YEAST
CORN

Per slice:	
calories	384
protein	8 g
fat	17 g
carbohydrate	55 g
calcium	70 mg
sodium	318 mg

For a gluten-free pie, use Raw Nut Crust, page 180.

Here's a delicious treat for breakfast, lunch, or dessert.

Easy Cheezy Danish

4 slices whole-grain or gluten-free rice bread

½ pound firm regular tofu, mashed

¼ cup pure maple syrup

1 tablespoon fresh lemon juice

1 tablespoon sesame tahini (optional)

½ teaspoon ground cinnamon

½ teaspoon vanilla extract

¼ teaspoon salt

Preheat broiler. Arrange bread in a single layer on a dry baking sheet. Combine mashed tofu and remaining ingredients in a bowl and mix thoroughly. Carefully spread mixture evenly on bread slices, covering the bread completely to the edge. Broil several minutes until golden brown. Serve hot or warm.

Per slice:	
calories	154
protein	6 g
fat	3 g
carbohydrate	27 g
calcium	48 mg
sodium	273 mg

FREE OF:
GLUTEN
NUTS
CORN

Tofu Whipped Topping (#1)

MAKES 1½ CUPS

This delicately sweetened dessert topping is reminiscent of fresh whipped cream.

1½ cups (about 12 ounces) mashed firm silken tofu

2 tablespoons organic canola or safflower oil (optional)

2 tablespoons pure maple syrup

¾ teaspoon vanilla extract

¼ teaspoon salt

Combine all the ingredients in a blender or food processor and process several minutes until completely smooth. Chill thoroughly before serving. Store in the refrigerator.

FREE OF: GLUTEN NUTS YEAST CORN	Per 2 tablespoons:	
	calories	32
	protein	2 g
	fat	1 g
	carbohydrate	3 g
	calcium	13 mg
	sodium	57 mg

Tofu Whipped Topping (#2)

MAKES 1½ CUPS

This incredibly easy whipped topping has a mesmerizing flavor. Let it be the crowning touch to all your confections.

1½ cups (about 12 ounces) mashed firm silken tofu

¼ cup pure maple syrup

1½ tablespoons hazelnut oil, walnut oil, or organic canola oil

2 teaspoons vanilla extract

Good pinch of grated nutmeg

Combine all the ingredients in a blender or food processor and process several minutes until completely smooth. Chill thoroughly before serving. Store in the refrigerator.

FREE OF: GLUTEN NUTS YEAST CORN	Per 2 tablespoons:	
	calories	74
	protein	2 g
	fat	3 g
	carbohydrate	10 g
	calcium	19 mg
	sodium	14 mg

Preparing flaky, whole-grain pastry is not particularly difficult—the secret is in the technique. Work quickly and handle the dough as little as possible to guarantee the flakiest results. Use this simple, delicious crust for any sweet or savory pie.

Per slice (1/8th):	
calories	140
protein	3 g
fat	8 g
carbohydrate	16 g
calcium	8 mg
sodium	2 mg

FREE OF: SOY NUTS YEAST CORN

Flaky Pie Crust #1

1½ cups whole wheat pastry flour

¼ teaspoon salt

¼ cup organic canola or safflower oil
   or nonhydrogenated vegan margarine

3 to 4 tablespoons cold nondairy milk or water,
   more or less as needed

Have ready a 9-inch pie plate. Combine flour and salt in a large bowl. Cut in oil or margarine using a pastry blender or fork until mixture resembles coarse crumbs. Sprinkle milk or water over mixture, tossing gently with a fork to lightly moisten the dry ingredients. The flour should be evenly moistened, not damp or soggy. With your hands, quickly form the dough into a ball, handling it as little as possible.

Place between 2 sheets of waxed paper and roll into a circle about 1 inch larger than the pie plate. Remove the top sheet of waxed paper. Carefully flip crust over and lay it in the pie plate with the dough against the plate. Working very carefully and gently, remove the second sheet of waxed paper. Ease the crust into the pie plate without stretching or tearing it. Trim the edges or turn them under to within ¼ inch of the rim and flute. Thoroughly prick the sides and bottom of the crust using the tines of a fork to keep air bubbles from forming under the surface.

To prebake crust (for pies that will be filled and then baked), place in a preheated 400°F oven for about 12 to 15 minutes, or until it turns a deep golden brown. Remove from oven and allow to cool before filling.

To fully bake crust (for pies that will be filled and chilled or baked very briefly), place in a preheated 400°F oven for about 20 minutes or until it turns a rich brown color and is crisp. Remove crust from oven, and allow to cool before filling.

Flaky Pie Crust #2

This light, flaky crust is perfect for all types of pies, from dinner to dessert.

1 cup rolled oats

½ cup unbleached all-purpose flour

½ cup whole wheat pastry flour

½ teaspoon salt

¼ teaspoon baking soda

¼ teaspoon baking powder

⅓ cup ice water

¼ cup organic canola or safflower oil

1 tablespoon fresh lemon juice

Have ready a 10-inch pie plate. Grind oats into a coarse meal in a food processor or blender. Place in a medium bowl and stir in the flours, salt, baking soda, and baking powder. In a separate small bowl, whisk together the ice water, oil, and lemon juice. Pour over flour mixture all at once, tossing lightly to moisten evenly. The dough might be slightly sticky depending on the moisture content of your flour. With your hands, quickly form the dough into a ball, handling it as little as possible.

Follow directions for crust #1.

Tip: Lightly moistening your countertop with water will help to keep the waxed paper from sliding.

FREE
OF:
SOY
NUTS
YEAST
CORN

Per slice (1/8th):	
calories	156
protein	4 g
fat	8 g
carbohydrate	18 g
calcium	16 mg
sodium	184 mg

Use this delicious crust with your favorite dessert pies and cheezcakes.

Per slice (1/8th):	
calories	202
protein	2 g
fat	15 g
carbohydrate	18 g
calcium	17 mg
sodium	1 mg

FREE OF:
SOY
YEAST
CORN

This delicious gluten-free crust is great for any no-bake dessert pie. Soft, plump dates with a smooth shiny skin will process most easily.

Per slice (1/8th):	
calories	253
protein	6 g
fat	19 g
carbohydrate	19 g
calcium	70 mg
sodium	4 mg

FREE OF:
GLUTEN
SOY
YEAST
CORN

Caramel Nut Crust

1½ cups finely ground pecans

⅓ cup quick-cooking rolled oats

1 tablespoon powdered kuzu, arrowroot, or cornstarch

½ teaspoon ground cinnamon

¼ cup pure maple syrup

2 tablespoons brown rice syrup

1 teaspoon vanilla extract

Preheat oven to 350°F. In a large bowl, combine pecans, oats, powdered kuzu or arrowroot, and cinnamon, and mix well. Add remaining ingredients, and stir until thoroughly combined. Press into the bottom and sides of an oiled 9- or 10-inch pie plate or the bottom of an oiled 8- to 10-inch springform pan. For pies that require further baking, bake just until set, about 8 minutes. For refrigerator pies, bake until lightly browned, about 10 to 12 minutes. Cool completely before filling.

Raw Nut Crust

1 cup walnuts

1 cup blanched almonds

¼ teaspoon ground cinnamon

¼ teaspoon ground cardamom

¾ cup chopped pitted dates

Grind nuts and spices in a food processor. Add dates and process several minutes until well combined. Stop to scrape down the sides of the work bowl as needed. Mixture is ready when it holds together when pressed between your fingers. Press firmly into the bottom and sides of a lightly oiled 9- or 10-inch pie plate or the bottom of an 8- to 10-inch springform pan (using water-moistened hands will help keep the crust from sticking to your fingers).

Graham Cracker Crust

1⅔ cups graham cracker crumbs

3 tablespoons granulated sugar

6 tablespoons nonhydrogenated vegan margarine, melted

½ teaspoon ground cinnamon (optional)

Preheat oven to 350°F. Combine all ingredients in a medium bowl. Press into the bottom and sides of a 9- or 10-inch pie plate or the bottom of an 8- to 10-inch springform pan. Bake until set and golden, about 8 minutes. Cool completely on a wire rack.

MAKES ONE 9- OR 10-INCH PIE CRUST

FREE OF: SOY NUTS YEAST CORN	Per slice (1/8th):	
	calories	181
	protein	1 g
	fat	11 g
	carbohydrate	20 g
	calcium	4 mg
	sodium	217 mg

Granola Nut Crust

1 cup rolled oats

½ cup flour (any kind; your choice)

½ cup ground walnuts or pecans

1 teaspoon ground cinnamon

½ teaspoon salt

¼ cup organic canola or safflower oil

¼ cup pure maple syrup

1 teaspoon vanilla extract

Preheat oven to 350°F. In a large bowl, combine oats, flour, nuts, cinnamon, and salt, and mix well. In small bowl or measuring cup, combine oil, maple syrup, and vanilla. Pour into oat mixture and stir well until evenly blended. Press into the bottom and sides of a 9- or 10-inch pie plate or the bottom of an 8- to 10-inch springform pan. For pies that require further baking, bake just until set, about 8 minutes. For refrigerator pies, bake until lightly browned, about 10 to 12 minutes. Cool completely before filling.

MAKES ONE 9- OR 10-INCH PIE CRUST

Try this spectacular crust for any sweet pie, including cream pies, fruit pies, or cheezcakes.

FREE OF: SOY YEAST CORN	Per slice (1/8th):	
	calories	153
	protein	2 g
	fat	8 g
	carbohydrate	19 g
	calcium	12 mg
	sodium	134 mg

MAIL ORDER SUPPLIERS OF SPECIAL INGREDIENTS

Ariël Vineyards
PO Box 3437
Napa, California 94558
phone: 800-456-9472; fax: 707-258-8052
www.arielvineyards.com

An impressive selection of award-winning, premium wine that has been de-alcoholized through cold filtration. Contains less than ½ of 1% alcohol and has no added sugar.

Bob's Red Mill
5209 SE International Way
Milwaukie, OR 97222
phone: 503-654-3215; fax: 503-653-1339
www.bobsredmill.com

Produces more than 400 products, from hot cereals to mixes to cornmeal to flour milled from all grains. Included in this astounding variety of grains are teff, amaranth, spelt, quinoa, and sorghum, as well as dried beans (including heirloom varieties) and bean flours.

Frontier Natural Products
PO Box 299 / 3021 78th St.
Norway, IA 52318
phone: 800-669-3275; fax: 800.717.4372
www.frontiernaturalbrands.com

A dazzling array of non-irradiated herbs, spices, extracts, and flavorings along·with related accessories. A good source for herbal seasonings, all-natural vegan bacon bits, and vegetable oils. Many products are available in bulk.

Gold Mine Natural Food Company
7805 Arjons Drive
San Diego, CA 92126
phone: 1-800-475-3663; fax: 858-695-0811
www.goldminenaturalfood.com

Offers a wide variety of top-quality, hard-to-find organic and heirloom foods, macrobiotic specialty items, top-quality kitchenware, natural body care, and eco-friendly household items.

Miss Roben's
91 Western Maryland Parkway, Suite 7
Hagerstown, MD 21740
800-891-0083 (outside continental USA: 301-665-9580)
www.missroben.com

Serves those with food allergies and intolerances, particularly those with multiple food issues. Sells many prepackaged products, as well as manufactures a complete line of mixes in their own plant to ensure no risk of cross contamination with gluten, wheat, dairy, egg, soy, or nuts. As a completely gluten-free, wheat-free company, no gluten or wheat is processed in the plant and no opened sources of dairy, nuts, soy, or eggs are allowed in the manufacturing section of the plant.

The Mail Order Catalog
413 Farm Road / Box 180
Summertown, TN 38483
800-695-2241
www.healthy-eating.com

Presents an extensive assortment of vegan pantry staples including nutritional yeast flakes, soyfoods and meat alternatives, tempeh starter, oils, nuts, seeds, nut butters, cereals, seasonings, mixes, and so much more. Also offers appliances and special products for gluten-free and allergy-free cooking.

REFERENCES

Bertron P, Barnard ND, Mills M. "Racial bias in federal nutrition policy, part I: the public health implications of variations in lactase persistence." *J Natl Med Assoc* 1999; 91: 151-7.

Centre for European Agricultural Studies and The European Forum on Nature Conservation and Pastoralism. "The Environmental Impact Of Dairy Production In The E.U." http://europa.eu.int/comm/environment/agriculture/pdf/dairy.pdf

Cumming, R.G., Klineberg, R.J. "Case-control study of risk factors for hip fractures in the elderly." *Am J Epidemiol* 1994; 139: 493-505.

Cummings, S.R., Nevitt, M.C., Browner, W.S., et al. "Risk factors for hip fracture in white women." *N Engl J Med* 1995; 332: 767-73.

Dairy Management Inc. www.dairycheckoff.com/news/release-012403.asp

ESHA. The Food Processor nutritional analysis program. www.esha.com

Feskanich, D., Willet, W.C., Stampfer, M.J., et al. "Milk, dietary calcium, and bone fractures in women: a 12-year prospective study." *Am J Public Health* 1997; 87: 992-7.

Got Milk? Campaign. www.whymilk.com/celebrities/index.htm

Grace Factory Farm Project. www.factoryfarm.org/cattle.html

Havala, Suzanne. *Good Foods, Bad Foods, What's Left to Eat?* Chronimed Publishing 1998.

Hertzler AA, Anderson HL. "Food guides in the United States." *J Am Diet Assoc.* 1974; 64: 19-28.

Huang, Z., Himes, J.H., McGovern, P.G. "Nutrition and subsequent hip fracture risk among a national cohort of white women." *Am J Epidemiol* 1996; 144: 124-34.

IDFA (International Dairy Foods Association) Letter to USDA Regarding Proposed Changes to WIC Program, 9/10/02. www.idfa.org/about/index.cfm

Karjalainen, J., Martin, J.M., Knip, M., et al. "A bovine albumin peptide as a possible trigger of insulin-dependent diabetes mellitus." *N Engl J Med* 1992; 327: 302-7.

National Dairy Council www.nationaldairycouncil.org/lvl04/nutrilib/newknow/nka1.html

Nestle, Marion. *Food Politics: How the Food Industry Influences Nutrition and Health.* University of California Press. Berkeley, 2002.

Nordin, B., Polley, K.J., Need, A.G.,et al. "The problem of calcium requirement." *Am J Clin Nutr* 1987; 45: 1295–304. [Medline]

Outwater, J.L., Nicholson, A., Barnard, N. "Dairy products and breast cancer: the IGF-1, estrogen, and BGH hypothesis." *Medical Hypothesis* 1997; 48: 453-61.

Pennington, J.A. *Bowes and Churches Food Values of Portions Commonly Used, 17th ed.* New York: Lippincott, 1998.

Physicians' Committee for Responsible Medicine. www.pcrm.org and www.pcrm.org/health/Info_on_Veg_Diets/dairy.html

Robbins, John. www.foodrevolution.org/racismfoodhealth.htm

Scott, F.W. "Cow milk and insulin-dependent diabetes mellitus: is there a relationship?" *Am J Clin Nutr* 1990; 51: 489-91.

US Department of Agriculture, Human Nutrition Information Service. The Food Guide Pyramid. *Home and Garden Bulletin.* No. 252. Washington, DC. August 1992.

USDA National Nutrient Database for Standard Reference, Release 15. www.nal.usda.gov/fnic/foodcomp/Data/SR15/sr15.html

U.S. Soyfoods Directory. Soymilk Calcium Chart. www.soyfoods.com/nutrition/CalciumChart.html

van Beresteijn, E.C., Brussaard, J.H., van Schaik, M. "Relationship between the calcium-to-protein ratio in milk and the urinary calcium excretion in healthy adults—a controlled crossover study". *Am J Clin Nutr* 1990; 52: 142–6

Weinsier, R. "Dairy foods and bone health: examination of the evidence." *Am J Clin Nutr.* 2000 72(3): 681-9.

Welsh, S.O., Davis, C., Shaw, A. *USDA's Food Guide: Background and Development.* Hyattsville, MD: United States Department of Agriculture, Human Nutrition Information Service; 1993. Publication Number 1514.

Work Group on Cow's Milk Protein and Diabetes Mellitus. "Infant feeding practices and their possible relationship to the etiology of diabetes mellitus." *Pediatrics* 1994 94: 752.

ALLERGEN-FREE INDEX

SOY-FREE RECIPES

NUT-FREE RECIPES

YEAST-FREE RECIPES

CORN-FREE RECIPES

ALL THE RECIPES IN THE BOOK ARE CORN FREE EXCEPT THE FOLLOWING:

INDEX

Philly Pot chowder 73

BOOK PUBLISHING COMPANY

since 1974—books that educate, inspire, and empower

To find your favorite vegetarian and soyfood products online, visit:
www.healthy-eating.com

also by Jo Stepaniak

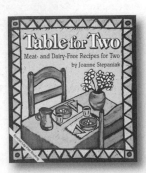

Table for Two
Meat- and Dairy-Free
Recipes for Two
978-1-57067-019-0 $14.95

Vegan Vittles
Second Helpings
Down-Home Cooking
for Everyone
978-1-57067-200-2 $19.95

Dairy-Free & Delicious
Brenda Davis, R.D
recipes by Bryanna Grogan
& Jo Stepaniak
978-1-57067-124-1 $14.95

The Saucy Vegetarian
Quick & Healthful No-Cook
Sauces & Dressings
978-1-57067-091-6 $15.95

Food Allergy Survival Guide
Vesanto Melina, MS, RD
Jo Stepaniak, MSEd
Dina Aronson, MS, RD
978-1-57067-163-0 $19.95

Food Allergies
Jo Stepaniak, MSEd
Vesanto Melina, MS, RD
Dina Aronson, RD
978-1-55312-046-9 $11.95

Vegan Deli
Wholesome Ethnic
Fast Foods
978-1-57067-109-8 $15.95

Purchase these health titles and cookbooks from your local bookstore or natural food store,
or you can buy them directly from:

Book Publishing Company • P.O. Box 99 • Summertown, TN 38483
1-800-695-2241

Please include $3.95 per book for shipping and handling.